NSYNC
30TH ANNIVERSARY
CELEBRATION

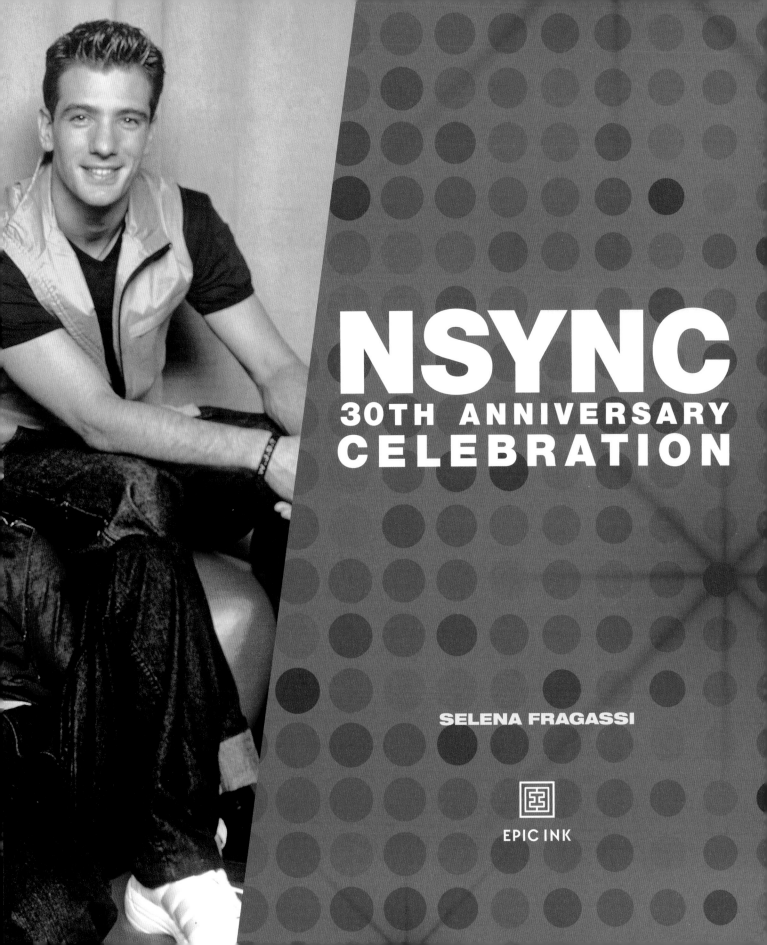

NSYNC
30TH ANNIVERSARY
CELEBRATION

SELENA FRAGASSI

EPIC INK

FOR THE FANS
WHO HAVE BEEN
PATIENTLY WAITING

CONTENTS

OPPOSITE: NSYNC in Germany in 1999.

PREVIOUS PAGE: Chris, Justin, Joey, Lance, and JC in Los Angeles in 1999.

Group photo shoot in Miami, Florida in November 2021.

INTRODUCTION

The other day when I was shopping in Whole Foods, NSYNC started playing over the speakers, and the song "Tearin' Up Heart" became the soundtrack as people picked up rotisserie chickens, felt around a pile of avocados, and stood in the self-checkout line gripping shopping baskets that looked ready to explode. Every single person was either bopping their head, tapping their feet, or mouthing the words—whether they were 25 or 55. It's been nearly 30 years since NSYNC came into our collective consciousness, and that moment made it clear, we have never forgotten them.

Even as the band went on a hiatus in 2002 that was only supposed to last a few months but lasted 20 years. Even as Justin Timberlake went on to forge his own musical path and become one of the biggest-selling solo artists of all time. Even as Lance tried to go to space, Chris tried to dress us like street punks with his clothing line, Joey stole our hearts as a *Big Fat Greek*, and JC made music of his own.

In all that time, fans kept up websites, wore the band's merch, repeatedly played the music videos, and every April 30 looked forward to the time they could say, "It's gonna be MAY!" They clung to every bit of news and sightings of the band together as evidence they were going to reunite officially, all but becoming an impressive community of internet sleuths. Even the fact that NSYNC's record for the most album sales in a week (2.41 million for *No Strings Attached*) wouldn't be broken for 15 long years says a lot—we've always wanted them, and now more than ever, we want them back.

And when Justin, JC, Joey, Lance, and Chris gave us all that glimmer of hope in September 2023 by reuniting at the VMAs, a time when even the holy mother of pop herself Taylor Swift had an unhinged freakout moment, something felt right with the world again. The mere chance that we might see a reunion and new tour from the five has had a seismic effect, proving that time, age, and absence makes no difference when you're a fan, especially a boy band fan.

NSYNC's story is full of affection, as beloved as the Disney roots they sprung from. Chris Kirkpatrick was singing doo-wop harmonies at an Orlando theme park and wanted to form an a cappella group, and the first kids he found were Justin and JC, who had both gotten their starts on *The Mickey Mouse Club*. Could it get any sweeter than that? Plus, they were a hodgepodge of personalities and upbringings who really had no business being in a group together. Justin, the Southern charmer from Memphis; JC, the incredible singer with the humble beginnings in Maryland; Joey, the hilarious Italian from Brooklyn; Lance, the closeted gay kid who grew up in a conservative Southern Baptist family; and Chris, who grew up in poverty in Ohio and Pennsylvania and always wanted to be an entertainer. But, oh, when they sang together, nothing sounded more perfect.

Unfortunately, the incredible desire of each of NSYNC's members to be stars brought them into nefarious hands, putting them at the mercy of their overlord, Lou Pearlman. Lou not only swindled his boy band members out of money but, behind the scenes, was also running one of the biggest Ponzi schemes in American history. Even before the FBI caught up with Lou and he was served a literal death sentence (he died of a heart attack in prison), NSYNC took him to court themselves, winning both their freedom from Lou and respect from so many. The result was one of their finest records and one of the biggest-selling albums of all time, the appropriately named *No Strings Attached*.

Though they got started in Germany (just like the Beatles and the Backstreet Boys), NSYNC was always a piece of American pie. They played a Super Bowl halftime show, became Chili's ambassadors, had lucrative deals with MSN at the dawn of the internet, were immortalized in Madame Tussauds, and even appeared on an episode of *The Simpsons*. They gave us the dance moves in "Bye Bye Bye" that we still practice to this day, embodied the very fabric of Y2K-core fashion, made frosted tips *the* look of the 2000s, and, in Lance's case, made the groundbreaking move to come out as gay at a time in America that the LGBTQ+ community wasn't as widely accepted.

And then it all went away, without any real explanation, a final tour sendoff, or at least an album sayonara, at the height of their celebrity. "Despite having one of the most short-lived boy band careers, NSYNC was arguably the most famous," says *Billboard*. "Backstreet Boys may have had the longevity, but *NSYNC had the glory," adds *Entertainment Weekly*, placing the band at the number one spot in their ranking of boy bands from the 1990s and 2000s.

So, yes, when they came out in their MTV best to present the pop award at the VMAs in 2023, there was good cause for a total freakout.

The guys have been teasing us with reunion rumors ever since, and we think there could be no "better place" for one than in this thirtieth anniversary year.

The boys photographed for *YM* in 2000.

PART I
HERE
WE GO

JC, Joey, Chris, Lance, and Justin
perform in Las Vegas in November 1999.

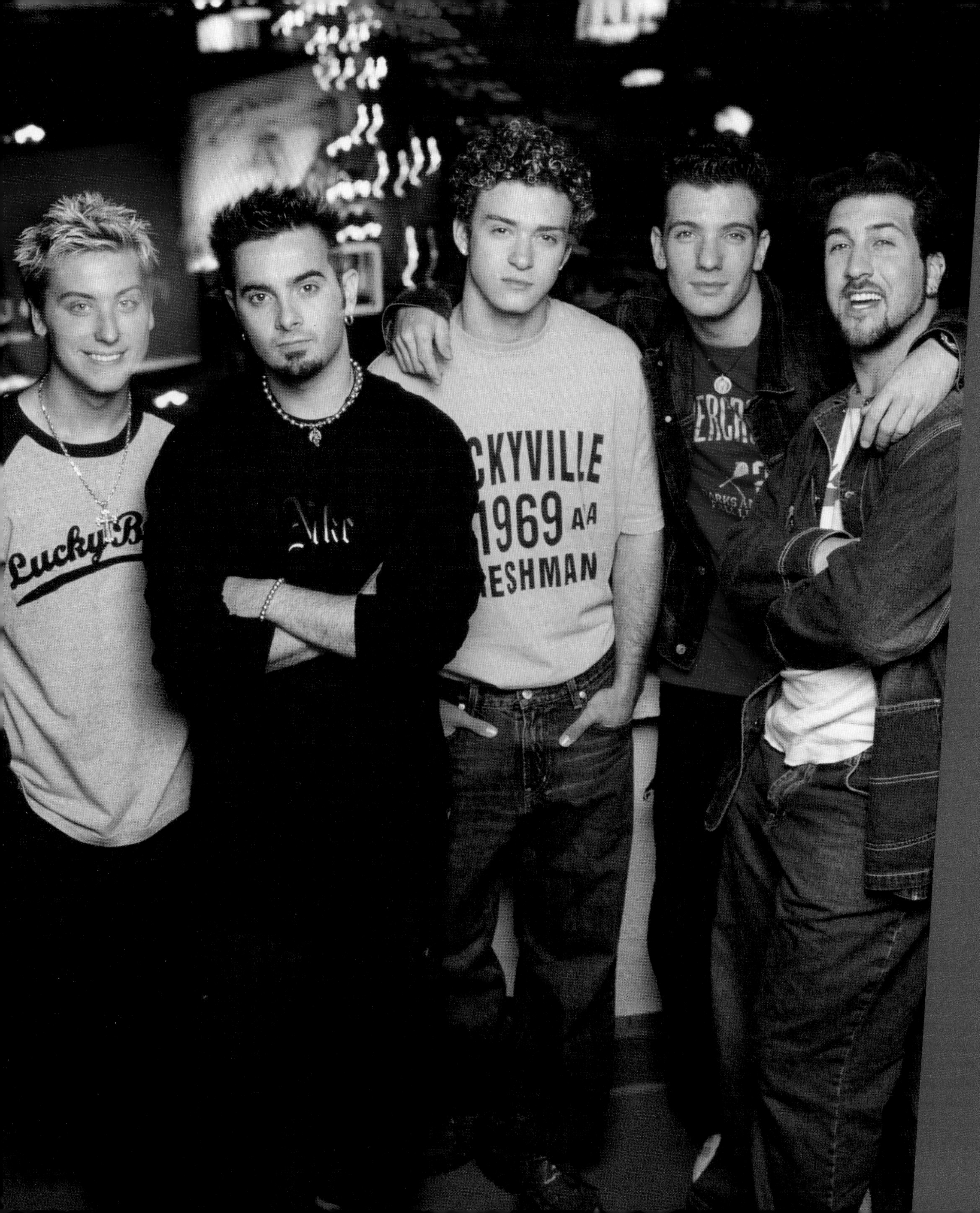
CKYVILLE
1969 AA
RESHMAN

1

A NEW GENERATION IS WAITING

"If no one knows the group NSYNC at that age, that's just bad parenting right there."

—Lance speaking to *Entertainment Weekly* about Gen Z

There are a chosen few that come around every generation to form that most beloved of musical acts: the boy band. The teen idols. The musical hook, line, and sinker that reels in fans and lives within them for decades to come, fueling their wistful nostalgia. In the world of pop music, history often repeats itself, but no more so than with the genre of boy bands. In the '60s, it was the Jackson 5; in the '70s, the Osmonds and Menudo; in the '80s, New Edition and New Kids On The Block; and in the Y2K era of the late '90s and early 2000s, it was an all-out explosion of acts, with the closely aligned Backstreet Boys (BSB) and NSYNC leading the pack, supported by groups like 98 Degrees and O-Town.

"From 1999 to 2002, NSYNC was everywhere, and they drove the girls crazy," an *A&E Biography* on the group begins. In fact, from NSYNC's start until they officially went on hiatus in 2002, the quintet became one of the biggest boy bands of all time with songs like "Bye Bye Bye" and the meme giant "It's Gonna Be Me." Their wild exposure also served as the foundation for one of modern music's

NSYNC at the Chateau Marmont in Los Angeles in January 2000.

biggest solo acts, Justin Timberlake. To understand the meteoric rise and lingering fascination that directly affected their unexpected regrouping at the VMAs in 2023 is to look at the history of the highly successful pop music machine.

According to *Dictionary.com*, a boy band is "a trendy pop group of young male singers, each member typically cultivating an image so as to appeal to a preteen audience." NSYNC— and their predecessors and contemporaries— all fit this carefully constructed mold. A big distinction in the genesis of boy bands versus other music acts is that the talents in these groups are all primarily vocalists (though some are also instrumentalists and/or producers), and each member is carefully selected not just for their vocal abilities but also for their dancing skills and proficiency for following orchestrated choreography. Each group also usually settles on five members.

Why five? Though we may never know the true reason, in numerology, five signifies curiosity and change, so maybe there were some astrologers in the boy band world who thought the number five was a good one to settle on.

Having a good "look" and fitting into one of the familiar boy band archetypes (i.e. the bad boy, the sensitive and innocent one, the athletic type, the oddball, and the baby of the group) is also a bonus. These archetypes also lead to the other hallmark of the pop music phenomenon— the uber-devoted fanbase.

If they weren't comprised of family members (as in the case of the Osmonds and the Jackson 5), many boy bands throughout history have been cobbled together through an audition process in which producers and managers put together the puzzle pieces. That's the other big trait of boy bands—the mogul, impresario, or Svengali figure behind the act, the proverbial great and powerful Oz behind the curtain. Back in the days of Motown, it was Berry Gordy; in the times of New Edition and New Kids On The Block, it was Maurice Starr. In the case of NSYNC and the 1990s/2000s crop of acts, it was the now-disgraced conman Lou Pearlman.

These architects are instrumental in the decision-making of their boy band machines and are incredibly savvy, if not also ruthless, in determining the course of the groups.

The Jackson 5 in 1977.

At best, they might have been the ones to scribe the music (or be accused of doing the actual singing, as in the case of Maurice Starr and NKOTB); at worst, like Lou, they found themselves accused of embezzlement and fraud and taking advantage of their curated cultural kingpins.

When it comes to K-pop, the current evolution of boy bands, there are sometimes full corporations behind the groups. Once band members sign a contract, they might be put through grueling training regimens, aka K-pop boot camp, sometimes working hard for years before they make their debuts on professional stages.

Not that it was much different for groups like NSYNC. In the 2019 film, *The Boy Band Con: The Lou Pearlman Story*, produced by Lance Bass, members of various groups like NSYNC, Backstreet Boys, and O-Town (all overseen by Lou) describe the ways the mogul turned them into nonstop workhorses.

"When Pearlman signed 'N Sync, he got them a house, told them they could quit their jobs and put them through a boot camp in unairconditioned airplane hangars," *USA Today* explains in an overview of the documentary. Pearlman's groups spent up to eight hours a day working in these brutal conditions. "I'm surprised none of us got

The Osmonds in 1973.

NSYNC in 1999.

heatstroke," Chris Kirkpatrick said in the film, though he added, "As repetitive and annoying as it got, it was fun."

And it was fruitful. NSYNC (and the concurrent career of the Backstreet Boys) filled a major gap in the boy band timeline. Following the collapse of New Kids On The Block in 1994—after lip-synching claims and Jonathan Knight quitting the group due to his panic disorder did the group in—there was near silence on the boy band front for several years. Eighties kids were growing up and their music tastes were changing. Rap and grunge were paramount in the early 1990s, edging out wholesome, kid-approved bands like NKOTB, who even started going by that acronym in an attempt to appear more mature and win back fans.

But there was hope for boy band fans later in the decade. As *Billboard* points out, "By spring of 1998, pop had seen a long-overdue resurgence after a Nirvana-driven

grunge era, thanks to the 1997 breakthrough of megapop groups Spice Girls, Hanson, and most importantly, the Backstreet Boys. With the stage set, another five-piece boy band named *NSYNC was ready to join the Top 40 scene stateside."

In the few short years after NKOTB's demise, a tumultuous time in which the death of Kurt Cobain rocked the world of grunge, there came a new class of pop music consumers: the Millennial generation. Gen X's kid siblings were clamoring for their own soundtrack; at the same time, the Disney Channel became a megaforce in youth culture, including acting as a pipeline to boy band and pop music stardom. Justin Timberlake and JC Chasez came from *The Mickey Mouse Club*, and well-known names like Britney Spears, the Jonas Brothers, Demi Lovato, and Selena Gomez were also all later alums of other various programs on the channel.

Y2K IS COMING

As the world braced for the once-in-a-lifetime turn toward the year 2000, both a panicked and a fresh-start mentality took over humanity. Or, as CNN succinctly put it, "As we looked to the year 2000—that monumental Y2K—we saw both apocalypse and rebirth."

Technology was a huge part of the new dawn, and NSYNC used it to their advantage (as evidenced by the TRL appearance below). In 2000, Microsoft inked a deal with the fab five to "plaster them all over their platform," according to *VICE*. It was meant to bring teenagers over to MSN from the then-dominating dial-up service AOL, all for the cool price of $21.95 a month. The NSYNC branding included browser wallpapers featuring photos of your favorite guy; web buttons that, once clicked, would play songs from the NSYNC catalog; and newsletters and exclusive news spilling all the band tea. The service was the 2000s-era version of the boy band hotline, souped up for discerning Millennial teens. And it came with a fat paycheck, potentially netting NSYNC $20–30 million.

NSYNC also teased the future of tech on the song "Digital Get Down" from *No Strings Attached*, a record that revolutionized Y2K pop, according to critics at *Billboard*. Not only was the record an early example of hiring massive hip-hop production teams and steering away from formulaic music by genre hopping, but it also was one that ushered in the digital music revolution. As CDs were slowly being phased out, the *No Strings Attached* tracks were being shared on services like LimeWire and Napster.

"Digital Get Down" was full of techy synths and innuendo-laden lyrics, with some wondering if the band was piloting the idea of digital hookups. The *New York Times* described the track as "the first boy-band album with a song about video cybersex—a clear indicator of post-pubescent consciousness," and *Rolling Stone* said it was a "crash course in wireless foreplay."

"What's funny is we joke that 'NSync invented Skype and FaceTime, but that's really true in a way," John Andosca, host of an NSYNC podcast, told *Rolling Stone*. "Back in 2000, video calls weren't even a thing—heck, most people didn't really have cell phones yet, so the idea about being able to 'get down' with someone through a video screen as if they were right there, was like something out of a movie."

Of course, there was also Y2K-core style, which NSYNC all but modeled: baggy pants, frosted tips, puffy jackets, track pants and sweatsuits, metallic and bedazzled everything. All the guys were missing were some crop tops and butterfly clips from Claire's. Justin, in particular, "epitomized the Y2K boy band look," says *ID*, "a flashy, larger-than-life take on men's fashion that drew equally from Euro-trash, streetwear, and kitschy Americana."

NSYNC performs at the Grammys in February 2000.

In fact, by 1997, the Disney Channel had completely changed its format from family-friendly programming to shows and brands that appealed to kids and adolescents between the ages ofseven and seventeen. Early 2000s hits like *Lizzie McGuire* and *Even Stevens* and more modern Disney fare like *High School Musical*, *Hannah Montana*, and *Camp Rock* are all examples. And what kids were watching on screens at home easily translated into a hunger for entertainment in the live and commercial space. Enter bands like NSYNC.

It's easy to see how NSYNC became so popular in the late 1990s and early 2000s. They were literally poster children for the desirable demographic. In fact, NSYNC's breakthrough in the US market, after first dominating Europe, came in a 1998 performance for the *Disney: In Concert* series that "blew us up," according to Lance Bass.

According to author Shaun Scott in his book *Millennials and the Moments That Made Us: A Cultural History of the US from*

1982–Present, there was another way in which the Millennial generation shaped NSYNC's stardom: "The country's heavily commercialized pop culture apparatus swooped in to fill the void left by overworked parents. And marketers learned to appeal to Millennials as a distinct demographic with an exploitable consumer profile." Furthermore, says Scott, "Millennials began to make their presence felt as consumers of pop culture. In the 1990s, Millennials spurred hundreds of billions of dollars of their parents' purchases."

If commercialization wasn't enough of a boon, the other game-changer for NSYNC in later years was the fact that, once they fired and sued Lou Pearlman in the late '90s, they took control of their sound and were more overtly tapped into the music styles of the time. Though NSYNC started off firmly rooted in bubblegum pop and European dance shtick, in large part due to their early international production team, later material, like the group's freedom album, 2000's *No Strings*

Attached, tapped into the highly popular hip-hop aesthetic, which all but "shook up the sound of Y2K pop," according to *Billboard*.

"The album, released three months into the new millennium, was a turning point for turn-of-the-century pop," the magazine added. "Before *No Strings Attached*, none of the major teen-pop albums of the era had featured guest rappers or [big] name producers from the R&B world, and virtually every one that came after did."

The shift was not only a sign of the times but also undoubtedly added years onto the group's lifespan, quite a feat in the tricky and temporary nature of the pop landscape. In fact, if Justin's solo breakaway hadn't been so polarizing for the band and fans, who knows how long NSYNC could've stuck around?

Their appeal never totally wavered. By the time NSYNC finally appeared as a solid unit again at the MTV Video Music Awards in September 2023, and two weeks later released "Better Place," their first new song in twenty-plus years, they made headlines like it was 1999 all over again, often to the tune of, "Millennials, this is our moment." Chatter immediately turned to, "When are they formally reuniting and how do we get tickets to the tour?" Even *Rolling Stone* posited that, if NSYNC toured again, they "would pack arenas and possibly even stadiums all over the world," adding, "it would be a very good idea for everyone involved."

The magazine also confirmed the generational pull that has long carried the careers of boy bands, claiming NSYNC is right in the prime of the "20-year rule of nostalgia," when the millennial fans of yore are clamoring to return to the music of their youth. "'NSync has been in the prime nostalgia zone for a few years now," theorized writer Andy Greene. "Their fans are quite eager to fork over big money to see them again."

NSYNC in the
Netherlands in 2001.

FINDING A WAY THROUGH THE BACKSTREETS

"Reflecting on things, it's cool to see what each of the bands did and how it all worked together. It really was this symbiotic relationship with Backstreet, 98 Degrees, us, and even O-Town and other bands that came in."

—Chris talking to *Variety* in 2021

To call the story of NSYNC's mid-'90s formation, early 2000s breakup, and 2023 quasi-reunion anything less than a roller-coaster ride would be putting it mildly. Then again, what more would you expect from the boy band that hails from the theme park capital of the world—Orlando, Florida? In fact, without the Orlando entertainment launchpads of Walt Disney and Universal Studios, we never may have come to know Justin Timberlake, JC Chasez, Joey Fatone, Lance Bass, and Chris Kirkpatrick, or the music they made together—70 million albums strong.

But there was something else in Orlando. Namely, a fellow Florida band clamoring for the top of the pop charts, the Backstreet Boys, and the infamous manager of both acts, Lou Pearlman. Though

Some patriotic flair from NSYNC in 1997.

Chris performs with
NSYNC in Germany
in 1997.

Lou pitted them against each other for some time, in the end he found himself with two highly successful music groups.

Getting to the roots of NSYNC requires a look into the one guy who pretty much made it all happen: Chris Kirkpatrick. Without his ambition to form his own music group and his perseverance, NSYNC would never have happened. As *Elle* magazine once astutely wrote in a tribute to the singer, "I maintain that nobody gives Chris Kirkpatrick enough credit."

Born October 17, 1971, in Clarion, Pennsylvania, Chris was raised by a single teenage mom who claimed he looked like another singer—Elvis—when he was born. Chris's parents split up when he was an infant, and his biological father was not in the picture throughout his childhood. Chris has said he and his mother "grew up together" and faced some hard times, such as when the family (including two other siblings) were living below the poverty line and on welfare programs. Yet in the background there was always the allure of arts and entertainment that kept his spirits high. Chris's first gig came when he was cast to play the lead in a high school production of *Oliver!*; he was in sixth grade at the time. He auditioned with an authentic British cockney accent, and the drama teacher knew he was the best fit.

Chris's mother, Beverly Ann Eustice, also recalls her son's early leadership skills. As soon as he was old enough to get a job, he did so, finding work as a grocery store bagger. Each week, Chris would bring home his paychecks and give them directly to his mother. Although she told her young son to keep some of the money for himself, Chris refused. "He just wanted to be the man of the house; he wanted to take care of things," Beverly shared in an

episode of VH1's docuseries *Driven,* featuring the backstory of NSYNC.

After the family relocated to Ohio, Chris continued participating in school theater productions, as well as singing in choirs, learning various musical instruments, and delving into sports for a time. One of the music groups that young Chris was a part of was the All-Ohio State Fair Youth Choir, which just so happened to open for New Kids On The Block at an early gig at the Ohio State Fair.

By the time Chris graduated high school in Dalton, Ohio, in 1990, he already had stars in his eyes. As listed in his yearbook, the budding talent's future plans included one day "being rich" and famous. So, when the opportunity came for Chris to relocate to the entertainment hub of Orlando, Florida, upon graduation, he took it. His biological father was living there at the time and, in an effort to start building a relationship, offered to have Chris move down to Florida and he would provide financial help for his college studies.

Chris enrolled at Valencia College, where he first had the acting bug, but he quickly set his sights on music, both in and out of school. He eventually earned an associate degree in music in 1993, and his extracurriculars also supported his career visions. One of the music groups he joined was the Hollywood Hi-Tones, a retro doo-wop singing group that took shifts performing outside the '50s-style Mel's Drive-In™ at Universal Studios. Chris's vocal abilities and chemistry within a singing group were already drawing a crowd at that early stage. "He would stand there and sing and little girls would just be like [mouth agape]," said fellow performer Jeremy James in an interview for *Driven*.

It's said that Chris loved the a cappella style so much he wanted to form his own project. While in college, he started writing his own original songs, trying them out at local Orlando coffeeshops when he wasn't working at SeaWorld or Outback Steakhouse.

There are stories that Chris intended to try out for BSB but he found out too late about the auditions to make the cut. But fate had its way, and Chris eventually did link up with Lou Pearlman. In later years, the boy band scion would become a disgraced convict with a soured legacy, having used his boy bands to fuel a deep Ponzi scheme. But in the '90s, he was the "it guy," the music mogul responsible for not only Backstreet Boys and NSYNC but also the multi-season *Making the Band* TV show and its inaugural winners, O-Town.

Lou first got a taste of the potential of the boy band empire by licensing charter jets from his company Trans Continental to acts like New Kids On The Block when they went on tour. Realizing just how many millions pop groups were bringing in, a proverbial lightbulb went off in Lou's head and he became obsessed with the idea of investing in his own crop of acts. As he really didn't know what he was doing initially,

Johnny Wright (center) with Joey and Justin in 2004.

BOY BAND WARS

Were they friends or foes? If you ask the members of Backstreet Boys and NSYNC today, they'll likely take a "the more, the merrier" approach and largely put the blame for their highly publicized rivalry on the media. (As one example, see the *Rolling Stone* article that begins with the headline, "Backstreet Boys Out of Sync: Casualties of the Boy-Band Wars.")

But there was something to the battle in the late '90s and early 2000s. "When they both came out, I was Team BSB and my two best friends were both Team 'N Sync and I made them convert. I think it got ugly and there were a few days we didn't talk at school but they came around. They saw the light," a fan named Nicole recalled to *E!*

Part of the issue was by design, with Lou Pearlman all but creating the friendly fire that continued to hang over the scene. In the 2015 Backstreet Boys documentary *Show 'Em What You're Made Of*, there is a clip of Lou showing BSB's Kevin Richardson a tape he recorded of NSYNC in 1995 and commenting on the newly formed group's talents. "It was almost like a betrayal," Kevin says in the film. "When we started out, we were like, 'Yeah, we're a team. We're gonna take over the world. There's nobody like us.' Then you find out, 'Well, actually there is somebody like you.'"

Lance recounted the debacle to *Billboard*, noting there was a race to be the first to breakout in America after both acts got their footing in Europe. "'Cause I knew the first one [to breakout in America] was gonna get the market—there was no room for two groups like that," he shared. "Lou promised us, 'Oh yeah, your song will be released before the Backstreet Boys,' and of course that was a lie."

At the time, the bands were truly on each other's toes, whether it was booking appearances on MTV's *TRL*, heading out on simultaneous tours (BSB had the Into The Millennium Tour at the same time NSYNC embarked on NSYNC In Concert/Ain't No Stopping Us Now Tour from 1999–2000), or climbing their way up the charts. Just as the Backstreet Boys' self-titled debut finally peaked on the American charts at No. 4 in late January 1998, along came NSYNC's self-titled debut, which hit No. 2 by October of that year.

And yet, "There was never any bad blood or anything like that," BSB's Howie Dorough told *Huffington Post*. "In the media, maybe, there was more of a competition between us all, but once again, they [NSYNC] were doing their thing, we were doing our thing. There was plenty of space for both of us. There still is for all the groups that are out there now. I'm glad to see a resurgence with all the other groups that are coming back out again. We're keeping pop music alive."

In fact, BSB's AJ McLean and Chris Kirkpatrick have buried their own personal hatchet (they once dated the same girl) and have even collaborated, most notably on the 2021 track "Air," part of McLean's side project ATCK (All the Cool Kids) that features various singers in guest spots. "I think boy band fights are in the same realm as hockey fights. You fight when you're on TV, but then when you're not, you get a beer together. Now we're really good friends," Chris shared with *Billboard*.

Even fans are making room for both boy bands in their heart of hearts. "I think time has healed the great divide between NSYNC and BSB fans," fan Nicole told *E!* "It felt like a war back then, but reminiscing like this has made me feel like we fought the good fight together."

Howie of the Backstreet Boys, circa 1995.

he even hired Johnny Wright (NKOTB's one-time road manager) to help steer the operation.

While the Backstreet Boys came about through an audition process (Lou put an announcement in the *Orlando Sentinel* in 1993 advertising tryouts), NSYNC was a bit more of an organic affair. Lou's second endeavor dovetailed with his need to find "another band to get the younger sisters of the girls he already hooked with Backstreet Boys," according to the *Driven* docuseries.

But rather than find a symbiosis and different target demos for each band, Lou did a curious thing with the concurrent acts he produced—he pitted them against each other, invariably creating a competitive race for the top of the charts. It was one of the first hints of Lou's insatiable greed—and it worked. By 2000, there was no beating Backstreet Boys and NSYNC at their game as they rotated spots atop the *Billboard* charts. As *Rolling Stone* surmised in a 2018 throwback story, "Pearlman, whether accidentally or on purpose, created the Beatles vs. Stones of the new millennium as the groups raced to become bigger than one another."

Manager Johnny Wright told the magazine that he and Lou "used to joke all the time that we were going to turn Orlando into the next Motown, but we were going to call it Snowtown—because we weren't doing it with R&B acts, we were doing it with pop acts. I guess you could say Backstreet Boys are the Temptations and 'N Sync are the Four Tops."

The two acts, who have long admitted there was no animosity and have put some of the blame on the media for creating their "rivalry," eventually did find common ground: in their late '90s battle with Lou for unpaid royalties and earnings. (More on that later.)

But how did Chris meet Lou? As the story goes, Chris already had an inside connection, as he knew BSB member Howie Dorough; a few years earlier, both had been enrolled at Valencia College and been part of the same choir. Chris tapped into that relationship to get a meeting with Lou. As Chris recalled to *Huffington Post,* "There was another kid, Charlie Edwards, who went and became a Backstreet Boy, and I guess he had a falling out with a producer and quit. He's the one who came to me saying that this guy Lou Pearlman was looking for another band."

Howie has echoed the story—and also taken some credit for the turn of events that shaped boy band history. "Chris, over the years, kept in touch with Lou and then, little by little, Lou and Chris started forming *NSYNC," he explained to *Huffington Post*. "Indirectly, I partially had something to do with it."

Lou "liked what he heard from Chris," according to Chris's mom, Beverly, and he made an offer Chris couldn't refuse: If Chris found the right singers to join him in the music project, Lou would finance it.

In Sync with NSYNC

NSYNC, and the NSYNC fandom, changed my life, from the friendships I've made (the best I've ever had, ALWAYS!) to providing the soundtrack nearly every step of the way since my teen years, bringing comfort and housing a thousand memories. Traveling, laughing, singing, and crying, creating snapshots forever in my heart and soul. There is nothing quite like being there from the beginning, and still supporting and enjoying them over two-and-a-half decades later, the same as on Day One!

Chris is one of my favorite humans, we have made memories together that are my forever favorites, posing in an iconic way (as only we can), and THE HUGS, OH, THE HUGS . . . There have also been the dances. The first one in 2004 to Nelly's "Hot In Herre" felt like my Cinderella moment; the most recent was last year set to Smash Mouth, which brought back a feeling I'd thrived on for many years and brought tears!

Each time we are together it feels to my fangirl heart like coming home again no matter how many years pass. As a woman with cerebral palsy, I oftentimes never felt seen, even sometimes still, and Chris has become a voice of encouragement though the years that saved me with more than just his music but with these moments, the words we shared, and the smiles we still bring to each other. It's a friendship *we* hold dear.

Rosebud Bunker

JULY 2004

OCTOBER 2022

FOUR MORE JOIN THE CLUB

"That's what I think is so unique about us—we weren't just friends, we all played a part. . . . The five of us, our voices [each serve a] purpose for this group, and it's all about the five-part harmony."

—Lance talking to *Billboard* in 2018

With Lou Pearlman's promising offer on the table, Chris hit the ground running in 1994–95, in search of the best group of singers he could find. In the beginning, the newly minted talent scout began his search by auditioning fellow members of various school choirs and singing quartets he had been in, and he had actually signed up a few of them before they all began dropping out as movement on the project stalled and other opportunities arose.

Chris went back to the drawing board and pivoted to a new, more bootstrap idea—making cold calls. As he told the *Bobbycast* music podcast in 2020, "I think I went through the paper or something like that and . . . I called like nineteen agents. I'm like, 'Listen, I'm putting together this group. . . . This is my number, this is my address.' Click."

Of those nineteen agents, one got back to him, and that agent just so happened to represent a kid named Justin Timberlake. Chris recalled the formative events, telling *Bobbycast* host Bobby Bones

The band in London in 1997.

that he remembered driving his beaten-up Nissan Sentra over to Studio Plaza in Orlando to meet the talent agent, who gave him a manila envelope that held a cassette tape and headshot of JT.

Upon popping the tape into the player in his car, Chris recalled, "I heard this voice and I'm like, 'Oh my god, this is unbelievable, this is better than anyone that's been in my band yet.'" Impressed, Chris then took the glossy photo out of the envelope to find Justin's mug staring back at him.

Chris quickly called Justin's mom, Lynn Harless, and remembered it being a "tough call." Justin was super young at the time, just fourteen years old, and was living in Memphis, Tennessee—not exactly near Orlando. "I was like, 'Hey, I'm this twenty-four, twenty-three-year-old guy, and I wanna put your fourteen-year-old son in a band with me,'" Chris joked with Bobby Bones.

Not that Justin wasn't already familiar with central Florida. Just months prior, he had been in the nearby city of Lake Buena Vista working on The All-New Mickey Mouse Club, a revival of the long-running Disney kids' show. He was included in a cast of future superstars like Christina Aguilera, his future girlfriend Britney Spears, actors Ryan Gosling and Keri Russell, and of course fellow NSYNCer JC Chasez, who was nineteen by the time he joined NSYNC and already a role model to young Justin.

As Christina Aguilera once revealed to Rolling Stone, the bond between JT and JC had blossomed on the Mickey Mouse Club set: "JC was the cool older guy, and Justin wanted to be just like him." (Justin was also good friends with Ryan Gosling, a Canadian, who lived with JT and his mom for a time in Memphis.)

Justin and his mom-ager, Lynn Harless, in 2001.

By the time The All-New Mickey Mouse Club was canceled and wrapped up filming in 1994, Justin and JC had already been making music together, recording demos in Justin's home in Memphis, and they had plans to relocate to Nashville and continue the venture. With this in mind, Justin and his mom, Lynn, made the suggestion to tap JC for the prospective music group that Chris was putting together. Maryland native JC flew to Florida for the tryout, and, in fact, was the future bandmate that Chris met first. "Lou went and picked JC up from the airport and they came to my work," Chris told Bobbycast.

The three new bandmates quickly gelled—Chris taking on a countertenor/falsetto range and JC and Justin representing first and second tenor, respectively, as well as melody. They started spending time bonding as a trio in Orlando, putting the bones of the group together while still searching for the other members that would round out the ensemble.

As the early genesis of NSYNC shows, the influence of Orlando and Disney on the band's future multi-million-dollar empire cannot be understated. It's a classic story of right place, right time, right entertainment brand. If not for the Mickey Mouse Club reboot filming in close proximity to Chris's newly adopted hometown, would NSYNC ever have existed as we know it today? And, without their first show at Disney World's Pleasure Island in 1995, would the band have continued to be given a stage?

As mentioned above, The All-New Mickey Mouse Club was an incredible pipeline of talent with many of the Mousekeeters—especially Britney, Christina, and the NSYNCers—going on to dominate both the late '90s/early 2000s cultural landscape and the Billboard charts. It was also via this foundational Disney show that Robin Wiley, the beloved vocal coach who worked with the Mousekeeters, came into the picture, eventually becoming NSYNC's trusted resource.

"I think the most exciting thing for me was always . . . the rehearsals, the practicing. That's where we were really finding ourselves," JC told *Disney News* in 2018 of the formative experience. (That same year, he rejoined the franchise for *Club Mickey Mouse*, making a cameo as the school principal.)

"For us, every day was the best day of your life. . . . And all of a sudden, I got to experiment singing these different styles . . . I [got] to find my voice in that three-, four-year period," JC said in that interview. "There was no animosity, there was no jealousy. It really was—whatever [one of the Mousekeeters] did, they just did it well. They made us feel comfortable, they made us feel like we could be ourselves, and I think that's why so many of us have thrived and have gone on to really step out and be confident in who we are."

Justin has echoed JC's sentiments about the show, telling the *Hollywood Reporter* in 2017, "We were at the age when you just soak in everything. We were taking acting classes, music classes, dance classes. We were learning how coverage and editing and cinematography work. And being put in front of a live audience, learning how to engage the crowd to get a laugh. Honestly, it was like *SNL* for children." His mom, Lynn, agreed, telling VH1's *Driven*, "The training that he got there over the first two years, I think it's probably the best thing that could've happened for him."

Adding to the serendipity of the band's creation, one night while out in Orlando at Disney World's Pleasure Island (the place NSYNC would return to for their first real gig), Chris, JC, and Justin randomly crossed paths

with then-eighteen-year-old Joey Fatone. Joey was the only member of NSYNC that Chris knew prior to forming the boy band—the two had worked at Universal Studios together for a period of time. A lightbulb went off in Chris's head upon encountering Joey again, knowing he was a natural baritone and would fill a much-needed role in the group.

"I was like, 'Hey, this is my buddy Joey! We both worked at Universal!' And JC was like, 'Yeah, we know him. He used to come to the *Mickey Mouse Club*,'" Chris told *Huffington Post*. "So we all knew each other and we were like, 'Hey man, we're putting together a group!'"

Joey was a quick yes. And as the story goes, he was the one to suggest the original fifth member, bass singer Jason Galasso. Jason was two years Joey's senior, and the two originally met while in the same choral group in high school. A couple years after graduating, Jason went to community college to pursue entertainment, even becoming an extra on the ABC TV show *Family Matters*, and then joining an early singing group with Joey that eventually disbanded.

The two parted ways for a short while, but as Jason recalled to *The Digital Get Down* (an NSYNC podcast), it wasn't that long after he got an alert on his pager (so '90s!) from Joey informing Jason that he may have a new opportunity in the queue. "Joey tells me that he had met these guys and wanted to know would I be interested. . . . they were putting together a guy group and wondered if I would want to come out and meet and maybe audition."

In addition to Joey, Jason was also already familiar with JC. "I used to hang around with *The Mickey Mouse Club* before that," Jason told the podcast. After agreeing to the opportunity, Jason met up with Chris,

Justin, JC, and Joey at what would become the infamous NSYNC house in Orlando. The five guys settled on trying out Boyz II Men's "End of the Road" to see how their voices might mesh. "It all locked in perfect," Jason recalled. What he most remembered of that initial meetup, however, was how young Justin was. But upon hearing JT belt out his parts, Jason said, "It didn't matter how old [he was]; he could sing his butt off."

The chemistry was short-lived, however, once Jason realized the type of music Lou Pearlman wanted NSYNC to make. "[At that point], I'm still trying to decide what I want to do, what direction I want to go in . . . I remember the first time that Lou Pearlman brought over some music that he was thinking . . . we were going to be doing. I come from an R&B, hip-hop background, that's my love, my heart, my soul. And Lou comes over with this European-style techno and I was just like, hmmm, okay."

At the time, Jason was concurrently in a second group that was working on more R&B-oriented music and he opted to stay the course with them. Jason admitted he "struggled with the vision" of NSYNC and "never wanted to be a teen idol." And on the day the five guys were supposed to sign a contract with Lou (a document described as "phone-book thick," and in which Lou had ostentatiously written himself in as a sixth member), Jason backed out. As he recalled to *The Digital Get Down*, "At the last minute I told Joey, 'I can't do it.'" Eventually, Jason left entertainment and became a mortgage broker in Florida.

Jason's departure left a gaping hole in the group, which was now devoid of a bass singer. He would eventually be replaced by sixteen-year-old Lance Bass, but as Chris

A promotional image of the *Mickey Mouse Club* cast, including JC (at the top of the stairs).

Justin in 1993, during his Mickey Mouse Club years.

recalled to *Bobbycast*, "It took us a whole year to find Lance." The four remaining members stayed the course and signed Lou's contract even without Jason's involvement. Still, Chris shared, "We knew we needed a bass."

Mississippi-based Lance Bass was a suggestion of Justin's then vocal coach; he nailed his audition and quickly inked a deal to become NSYNC's fifth member. During Lance's audition at the Orlando NSYNC compound, Chris remembered high-fiving Justin as they listened to the new tryout's session. "Lance just kept going lower and lower and lower, and I thought, man, this is unbelievable," Chris told *Bobbycast*. Justin's mom, Lynn, also remembered that everyone in the room "had hairs standing up on the back of their neck" when hearing the newly minted five-piece group sing together for the first time.

With the final lineup intact, it was a near-perfect melding of voices and personalities. As Joey joked with *Huffington Post*, "We were never like, 'You have to be the funny one, you have to be the cool one, you got to be the sexy one.' . . . Chris is always the prankster and the jokester. Justin has a great voice and everyone wants to marry him. And the moms wanted to take me home and cook me dinner. That's the one I always got."

But there was some truth to the character development of each band member as time went on and as their personas grew, with each bringing a unique background to the mix. In addition to Chris's artsy/quasi bad boy aura explored in the last chapter, the background of the other four guys—from Southern gentleman Lance to tough New Yorker Joey—is just as intriguing and ties NSYNC together in perfect harmony.

THE YOUNG HEARTTHROB: JUSTIN

He may have been the youngest member of NSYNC, being just fourteen years old when he signed on, but Justin Timberlake was also one of the savviest, later knowing when to walk away from the project and capitalize on his solo fame. But his origins were much more humble. Justin Randall Timberlake was born January 31, 1981, in Memphis, Tennessee, to parents Randall Timberlake and Lynn Harless. His mom was an integral part of NSYNC in the early days, suggesting Justin's Mousekeeter pal JC join the band and giving the group its name (see the sidebar). His father, on the other hand, ran the choir at a local Memphis Baptist church. He also became an important cog in the eventual music career of his son, not the least of which was giving Justin his first taste of singing as part of the church choir.

At home, musical influences were part of Justin's foundation, as much a part of daily life as eating breakfast. Frequently spun albums included those from the Eagles, Stevie Wonder, and Marvin Gaye. Justin's uncle was also in

harmony to the radio?'" By the third grade, friend Trace Ayala remembered that he, Justin, and three other childhood friends had a group that would mimic and cover New Kids On The Block songs for school variety shows, all but inking Justin's future boy band destiny. Raw video footage from 1990 shows little JT already finding his dance moves and schoolgirls shrieking at the sight. "All of a sudden he was like, 'That's it, I found my mission in life. I'm seven years old and I know what I'm going to do with my life'," mom Lynn recalled in *Driven*. "That's when I knew there was something to this, he had something that was a little different."

Vocal lessons soon followed, where JT was deemed to be a "natural" by early coach Bob Westbrook. By eleven, Justin had begun his journey into the tenuous world of being a child star, appearing on the popular televised talent show *Star Search* in 1992. He lost in the first round but, just a short time later, in 1993, he was picked up for *The All-New Mickey Mouse Club*, which is where his whirlwind career went into overdrive—before *he* could even drive. "I think we can all agree that I did not have a normal childhood," Justin once told *The Hollywood Reporter*, while contemplating how to raise his own children (he shares two sons with his wife, actress Jessica Biel). "I have some faint images from my childhood, but no, I can't really remember not being famous."

Justin's parents split when he was a young child, but both remarried and gave the music star a brood of half-siblings; one of them, sister Laura Katherine, died shortly after she was born in 1997, the same year NSYNC put out their debut album in Europe; she is credited in the album acknowledgments as JT's "angel in heaven."

a bluegrass band, and his grandfather (who taught young JT how to play the guitar) once played with Elvis Presley and was a huge fan of country icons like Willie Nelson and Johnny Cash. And then, of course, there was the ripe background of Memphis itself—an epicenter of the blues—that filtered into the budding talent's expanding repertoire.

Though mom Lynn recalled to VH1's *Driven* docuseries that, as a child, Justin "never wanted to be touched [and] never wanted to be talked to . . . he wanted [people] to get out of [his] space," that of course would all change as he became one of the most recognizable and sought-after figures in pop music.

Justin's talent was unmistakable as a child. As Lynn recalled, "He was about two years old and we were driving down the street and my brother said, 'Has anybody noticed he's singing

JC and NSYNC perform as part of the Big Help Concert in 1999.

THE CONSUMMATE ENTERTAINER: JC

Before he took on the JC moniker, Joshua Chasez was born August 8, 1976, in Bowie, Maryland, just outside Washington, DC, and grew up in a very "ethnically mixed neighborhood," according to his mom, Karen, who also spoke to VH1 for *Driven*.

JC was the oldest of three children, raised in the Mennonite faith by Karen and Roy Chasez, who adopted the young boy when he was just five years old. While JC never knew his biological father, he was reared early on by his birth mother, who struggled and was often homeless; she ultimately chose to give

her child a better chance by relinquishing custody. As JC told KZZP-FM, "It [was] like, 'He's five years old. This kid needs to be in school. He needs something steady.' And as much as she loved me, [she] had to make the choice of basically separating herself as the day-to-day mother in order to give me a better life."

As dad Roy recalled to VH1, he and Karen knew JC had a "perfect ear" after they discovered their child would repeat things from the radio and would sing at family gatherings with perfect pitch (it's largely for this reason that JC has often been considered the strongest voice in NSYNC by both fans and even band members). Yet as a youngster, he was very shy and didn't like performing in front of other people.

Although, he started coming out of his shell in middle school, when he and his friend Kacy would perform synchronized dance routines at house parties. That eventually led to the friends joining a national dance competition called *Starpower*, where they nabbed first place for a routine set to M.C. Hammer's famous track, "U Can't Touch This."

JC's impeccable dancing skills were one of the facets also noticed by Matt Casella, casting director for *The All-New Mickey Mouse Club*, when JC auditioned for the Disney reboot. (Karen had seen an advertisement in the *Washington Post* for tryouts and urged her teenage son to go for it; it was his first audition ever.) "It was like hip-hop, funky, rap, and he went to town," Matt recalled of JC's tryout in *Driven*. The casting director was also taken with JC's vocal capabilities after he aced an audition with Richard Marx's "Right Here Waiting." As vocal coach Robin Wiley remembered, "JC was really, really talented and didn't know it."

Landing on Season 4 of *The All-New Mickey Mouse Club*, it was not only an important time for JC in terms of building his confidence and for the fateful friendship with Justin, but also for giving him his moniker. As there was already a Josh (Ackerman) cast on the show, producers opted to call the new guy JC—and the name stuck.

When JC was approached by Justin about the opportunity in Orlando, JC was hesitant at first, thinking that college may be a better path forward. But his dad pushed him to go for it: "I said, 'Josh, you know you don't want to be forty years old and say, "I wish I woulda tried."'"

JC performing with NSYNC on *The Tonight Show* in November 1998.

THE LOVABLE GOOFBALL: JOEY

As copious baby pictures of him show, Joseph Fatone Jr. has basically been smiling since birth, and he has kept that affable, goofy attitude throughout the NSYNC years and beyond. Born January 28, 1977, Joey was a bit of the odd man in the bunch. He didn't appear on *The Mickey Mouse Club* and wasn't found through talent agents or vocal coaches; it stemmed from a chance Orlando run-in with his former Universal Studios singing buddy Chris Kirkpatrick. Yet, without him, NSYNC would've never had their literal Y factor.

Joey and Justin at *Teen People*'s first anniversary party in 1999.

Joey grew up in the New York borough of Brooklyn (specifically the Bensonhurst neighborhood), part of a middle-class Italian family with big accents and big hearts. He was the youngest of three children and attended St. Mary's Mother of Jesus Catholic school where his class clown antics often got him in hot water with the nuns. "He was very fidgety and always getting into trouble," a former classmate told VH1.

At home, Joey's parents would film bits and sketches he put together, and his father helped foster an emerging love of music. In fact, Joe Sr. was part of his own '50s/'60s-style doo-

wop group back in the day called The Orions. "That's how [the siblings] got influenced, listening to '50s [music]," Joey told CNN's Larry King. "[My dad] was always supportive, always trying to do something creative."

Of all the Fatone kids, Joey was the one who was clearly interested in following in his father's footsteps. "Music was definitely his thing," brother Steven told VH1. "He was never shy." The family was one of the first in the neighborhood to have cable TV, and Joe Sr. recalled that his son was always watching MTV and trying to learn new dance moves. "He was a good dancer . . . and a good charmer too," Joe

Sr. shared with VH1, remembering the girls that would often ring the doorbell looking for Junior.

When Joey was thirteen, the Fatone family uprooted and moved to Florida. The family experienced major culture shock living in the Sunshine State after inner-city life, but Joey truly thrived. In high school, he took classes alongside *Mickey Mouse Club* member Jennifer McGill, with whom he formed a fast friendship.

Soon enough, Joey was part of the choral program, where a few of the students decided to take things outside school and formed a group called The Big Guys (one of the other members just so happened to be a teenager named Luis Fonsi, who would go on to be a huge Latin music star). The band often got gigs and shot a music video—at Universal Studios, where Joey later crossed paths with Chris as both logged time with their respective retro-tinged a cappella groups. Joey was also hired to be the "Wolfman" in the "Monster Show" at the theme park, where his acting chops came into play.

In addition to music, Joey took an early liking to theater and was involved in a number of high school productions, including *The Music Man, Damn Yankees,* and *West Side Story.* It was a talent that would come to be fruitful in later years, too, as an adult Joey made it to the Great White Way with a number of Broadway productions.

Beyond being the essential baritone in the group, Joey had another role: NSYNC's default documentarian. He carried his childhood practice of making at-home movies of skits and musical numbers over to the new group as NSYNC got going.

"Joey brought a video camera [every-where]—this was the age before camera phones. . . . And it wasn't just something like,

'Oh, that looks cool. Let me pull out my phone and record that.' This was making a conscious effort of, 'OK, we're doing this, let me film this' . . . he'd tape a lot of stuff," Chris told *People*.

As far as what he captured, Joey also shared with the magazine, "I have stuff from when we were doing the actual photos of our *Celebrity* album. I have video footage of all of us doing the stuff in the grocery store on the cover, and then all the inserts where we were making the breakfast. . . . I have one where Bill Clinton is playing the saxophone and BB King is playing guitar, which I don't even know what that was when we were doing [it]."

As the guys approach their probable reunion, having that footage is nothing short of priceless.

Joey and his camera during NSYNC's Challenge for the Children celebrity basketball game in 2002.

Lance photographed at os Angeles's Chateau Marmont in January 2000.

THE SHY GUY: LANCE

Like many other stargazer kids, when Lance Bass was little, he wanted to grow up to be an astronaut. But life had other plans for him—namely, joining a boy band who would go on to have astronomical success. Lance was the last one to come on board with NSYNC after early member Jason Galasso quit the group in 1994. It took a whole year of searching for the band to find their missing piece.

"We were calling everybody we knew, trying to see if anybody knew a kid who was like sixteen and could hit a low F," NSYNC vocal coach Robin Wiley recalled to VH1. The band had a showcase booked and demo recordings pending and really needed to find the right person to fill the gap in the band.

Enter Lance, who came as a recommendation from Justin's early vocal coach, Bob Westbrook; with studios in Memphis and Jackson, Mississippi, Bob had previously worked with both boys. "I gave [Justin] one name—Lance Bass," Westbrook told the *Clarion Ledger* about being asked to help.

As Justin recalled to CNN's Larry King, "[Bob] gave us Lance's name, and he said, 'But his mother will never let him do it.'" Lance knew it would be a hurdle to convince his parents too: "I didn't think my mom would ever let me do it!" he divulged to *Huffington Post*.

Born May 4, 1979, in Laurel, Mississippi, and raised in a conservative Southern Baptist household along with his older sister, Stacy, becoming a boy bander wasn't exactly the vision James and Diane Bass had for their son. Working in the medical and education fields, respectively, Lance's parents were much more supportive of his NASA dreams (they even took young Lance to Cape Canaveral when he was nine years old to see a space shuttle launch).

With some convincing—including Justin's mom, Lynn, calling Diane several times for mom-to-mom chats—eventually fate had its way. "He was a real sweet kid, good teenager, never got into any trouble," Diane told VH1. Sure enough, Lance became known as the shy, quiet one of the group who didn't ruffle feathers. "He was the one who turned beet red when the others mentioned girls, and put his hands over his face when the others got especially embarrassing," says fansite *Still NSYNC*.

Ultimately, Diane caved and allowed Lance to try out: "You just feel like you have to give him that opportunity, it doesn't come around every day," she later said. She would also soon join the band on the road and at rehearsals,

WHAT'S IN A NAME?

It's been written as NSYNC, *NSYNC, NSync, and 'N Sync—and there's just about as many stories of the band name's origin as there are ways to spell it.

One of the most well-regarded stories is that the idea for the moniker came from Justin's mom, Lynn. "The first time we sang together, she goes, 'Man, you guys sound really in sync.' And we were like ding, ding, ding," Justin told CNN's Larry King. The unique acronym then came from combining the last letter of each guys' first name: JustiN, ChriS, JoeY, JasoN, and JC.

When Jason left and Lance came in, that "e" at the end of Lance's name didn't exactly keep with the formula, but that was just a minor detail easily fixed by changing his name to Lanceton. Seriously— *Lanceton.* "They did call me Lanceton for a good year, just basically as a joke," the fifth member divulged to *Entertainment Weekly.* "I think it was Justin who first was like, 'Okay, Lanceton.' Then it kinda faded out once we got a deal. It didn't stick very long." But the band name did.

There's also an interesting backstory when it comes to that sometimes-used asterisk. It was apparently a "prophecy" of a British illusionist and magician by the name of Uri Geller. When NSYNC was getting rooted in Europe, they went to one of Uri's performances and chatted with him backstage after.

"We saw him in the UK . . . And he goes, 'I see something. It has to do with suns or stars or something with astronomy in your career.' And it's funny, a year later when we did the first album, for America, the [label] had [put] a star in [our name]," Joey shared with *Huffington Post.*

Uri confirmed the long-rumored myth to the outlet, saying, "I told them, if they place that star on their first CD, they're going to shoot up to No. 1." (It *almost* did, ultimately landing at No. 2 on the *Billboard* charts). Though Uri conceded, "I think drawing and writing down their name and creating that star gave them that subliminal push to go for it."

In a more tender moment, during NSYNC's Hollywood Walk of Fame Star ceremony in 2018 (pictured at right), JC went as far as to say the apostrophe in the band's name (apparently they prefer 'N Sync) was representative of their longtime vocal coach and erstwhile sixth member, Robin Wiley, who sadly passed away in 2006. "She is truly who made us who we are," JC said.

along with Justin's mom, Lynn, until the two
youngest members were legal adults.

But, when Lance did join NSYNC, he wasn't
exactly a natural fit. Sure, he could sing (Bob
Westbrook said Lance's voice changed very
early, leading to that coveted deep register),
but Lance had two left feet and struggled with
the band's intense choreography early on.
And he was not exactly a pop fan. "He loved
country, like Garth Brooks . . . Reba McEntire
was his first concert," a boyhood friend
revealed to VH1. That concert was a game
changer for little Lance, spurring his interest in
music, which had first ignited while singing in
his church choir.

Lance soon joined the Mississippi Show-
stoppers (a music program sponsored by the
Mississippi Agriculture and Forestry Museum)
as an extracurricular when he was in eighth
grade. And, upon becoming a freshman in
1994, he auditioned and was accepted into
Attaché, an award-winning show choir at
Mississippi's Clinton High School. It was
during his sophomore year in the program
that he and his mom got the call from Justin
and Lynn—and all the pieces fell into place to
create one of the most successful boy bands
in music history.

With the five members of NSYNC fully
assembled by 1995, it was time to get to work.
Doing so included spending time rehearsing
at a newly-purchased NSYNC compound,
recording in Shaq's house (yes, *that* Shaq),
and getting some new passports, as the boy
band first headed overseas to try to drum up
international interest in their pop music.

Justin, Joey, and
Lance matching
in Boston in 1998.

OFF TO EUROPE

4

"We started out in Europe. It got really big over there for us.
Then we would come back [to America] and there'd be nothing.
It was like we were two different groups."

—Lance talking to the *Clarion Ledger* in 2018

With the ink still fresh on the contracts, NSYNC entered their incubation period, a time in which they were to focus on NSYNC 24/7 to develop their sound, style, and voices. They didn't really know it in 1995, but the moment they put their John Hancocks on Lou's legal documents, Justin, JC, Joey, Chris, and Lance basically signed a deal with the devil. That deal would be described as a "web of robbery" in later years, with Lou pilfering profits to fund his own nefarious $300-million Ponzi scheme, which landed him in prison and led to multi-million-dollar lawsuits waged on both sides.

But, in 1995, everything was a proverbial paradise meant to distract the five guys (and their parents) from really understanding what was happening behind the scenes. They were, for all intents and purposes, the puppets on the strings they'd allude to in "Bye Bye Bye."

Lou basically promised the boy banders the same riches he flaunted in their faces. "When you meet Lou you immediately trust him for some reason. He had . . . a jolly personality . . . you felt like he was family," Lance, in retrospect, told ABC's *20/20* in 2019. "And when you see Lou . . . with his Rolls-Royces and limos and his beautiful mansion . . . you trusted that he knew what he was doing just because of all the things he had."

NSYNC photographed in Germany in 1997.

There were continual invites to parties and hangouts at Lou's giant Orlando home, one that mirrored the theme parks in the background of the city. Ashley Parker, a member of Lou's other boy band project, O-Town, compared the mogul's compound to Disneyland, recalling in the 2019 documentary, *The Boy Band Con: The Lou Pearlman Story* (produced by Lance Bass's company) that the sprawling grounds offered a movie theater, pool, and even WaveRunners. And Lou always offered up his giant, fun abode to any of his minions who wanted to throw their own party. As Backstreet Boys' AJ McLean says in the exposé, "Nick [Carter] and I had a double birthday party at Lou's house. It was a pool party, we invited all our friends. . . . He made himself more relatable to us by being this grown-up kid."

Lou promised his NSYNC guys all this and more, and even financed their own rental house, telling them to quit their menial day jobs. He'd pay the bills; all they had to do was focus on the band.

"He rented us our house, so we didn't have to pay for [it]. He would pay for dinners when we would go out . . . He's family to you. He's taking care of you," Lance recalled to *20/20*. That house was even described as a "commune" by Justin's mom, Lynn, a place where the five could live, work, and play together. "They had toys, basketball courts, and skate ramps." Not only that, but Lou gave each guy an allowance.

Vocal coach Robin Wiley remembered trying to get the guys to focus in between all the shenanigans. "Four of them would be playing video games, and I'd be in there teaching one of them their part, and I'd say, 'Okay, you're done. Go get Joey.' And then Joey would come in and Lance would take over his joystick at

Lou's home in 2007.

the video game," she shared in VH1's *Driven* episode. But the guys were also incredibly hardworking, sometimes rehearsing up to eighteen hours a day. A schedule would be posted on the wall in the house each day letting the guys know the run of events. And often that included working in the airplane hangars where Lou would otherwise store the jets in his Trans Continental Airlines fleet.

The rehearsals were relentless, often described as a "bootcamp." The hangars weren't air-conditioned either, giving new meaning to the "sweat" in the "blood, sweat, and tears" put into the effort to become a chart-topping music group. There were choreographers, voice sessions with Robin, and tutors for Justin and Lance, who had yet to graduate high school in 1995.

There were also early recording sessions at basketball legend Shaq's house. During the '90s, when he was a superstar player for the Orlando Magic, Shaq's monstrous mansion had a guest house outfitted with a recording studio called TWISM (The World Is Mine). That was where NSYNC recorded their first demo tracks. "It was kind of our first break," JC told *Billboard*. Prior to using Shaq's state-of-the-art recording facilities, NSYNC had laid down tracks like early numbers "Sailing" (a cover of Christopher Cross) and "Giddy Up"— both of which would appear on their self-titled debut—with their early producer Veit Renn in ramshackle spaces the size of small closets, with mattresses on the walls for soundproofing.

As the story goes, Shaq heard NSYNC sing the national anthem at a sporting event and approached the guys to find out who they were. "We said we were a new group, and we were looking to put our demo together, and he offered his studio to us. It was a very

Shaquille O'Neal in the 1990s.

generous offer, and we took him up on it," JC shared. Though Shaq wasn't ever at the studio when NSYNC was using it, the opportunity was a prime moment. "Walking into Shaq's place, I think the thing that felt good was, 'OK, this is the first person that sees something. They see what we see. We feel like we have something, and now someone else recognizes it,'" JC added. And with the

NSYNC with Johnny
Wright (center) at
their Walk of Fame
ceremony in 2018.

music recorded there, the band then used that demo to try to get labels interested in the project.

As the five members of NSYNC were working themselves to the bone to produce a boy band that Lou would continue to

finance, the mogul also implored them to keep everything under wraps. As Chris told *20/20*, "It was always like a secret. Like, everything was, you know, 'I'm doing this, but I'm also working with them [Backstreet Boys]. So don't tell anybody about this. Don't say that I'm involved with you. Don't say that you really even know me, but I'm going to try to help you guys out.'"

In talks with Backstreet Boys road manager Johnny Wright (who would go on to become NSYNC's manager), things were even more shady. "I called Lou and I was like, 'You have another boy band I don't know about?' He was, 'No, no, no.' He goes, 'This kid Chris Kirkpatrick . . . wants to put a band together and he just comes to me every once in a while to ask for some advice, but I got nothing to do with that band,'" Johnny told *20/20*. It was the first in a long series of Lou's many red flags.

Even so, all pistons were firing to rev up NSYNC and find them a record deal. There was just one problem—no one in the US was buying into it. While the band was signed to Lou's Trans Continental Records, they still needed major label representation for distributing their music and getting it out to the masses, and that required getting one of the big record houses to pony up.

But, "every record exec out there turned us down," Lance told *20/20.* "They were like, 'Nothing like this would ever work in America. This is way too cheesy.'" At the time, grunge and hip-hop ruled the charts. Not to mention the fact that many decision makers believed there was only room for one high-level boy band in the US and that spot had already basically been filled by the Backstreet Boys, who were making themselves known in the mid-1990s.

NSYNC was still trying to invent itself and hone in on a sound that combined their love of a cappella with more modern, catchy flair. Chris called it "dirty pop," and described it to *People* as "this whole new way of using the same sounds from the older pop days, but making it new. . . . It was still very bubble-gummy, but it wasn't your parent's bubblegum." More simply,

Lance said they were a "vocal R&B group" that idolized Boyz II Men and tried to emulate their style. And Justin told *Billboard* that he believed "our voices bring a real R&B feel to pop tunes." But nothing about that screamed "fresh and hip" to music execs. It was more of a "been there, done that."

If the music wasn't sitting well with music executives, NSYNC's image was even more of a sore spot. The baggy jeans, the bedazzled sporty wear, the obsession with denim, and the sweaters several sizes too big came off as "clownish," per *Huffington Post.* And for their big day out in New York City, to take meetings with record honchos? The guys bought puffy silver vests and bugged-out sunglasses that made them look like some kind of human-sized, space-age insects.

"Our clothes were just horrible," Lance has said, laughing off those early days. "They were always just oversized. No one really cared. There was no stylist that came in and was like, 'Oh we're going to do this and we're going to fit you.' No, it was, like, 'Here's a rack of stuff.'" Furthermore, as he told *Huffington Post*, "We didn't really have a choice of what we wore at the beginning because it was just whatever we could afford." Though Chris remembers there was at least *some* functionality behind the fashion: "I remember we wore these skintight shirts, big black baggy jeans, and black combat boots. But at the time, it was the easiest thing to dance in," he told *People.*

And then there were the promo shots. Since coming back together at the 2023 VMAs and causing a pop world uproar, the band has been having a ball making light of the saccharine early days. "Who had us pose like that?!" they posted on social media, alongside a recreation of a heyday photo.

But there *was* a market for what they were selling: Europe. In the mid-'90s, boy bands were huge on the continent, particularly in Germany. Following in the footsteps of the Beatles, whose long residency at a club in Hamburg in 1960 helped them garner attention back home in the UK, and the Backstreet Boys, who also became German phenoms before they were American heartthrobs, NSYNC took the same course.

It all started with the band's very first live showcase in October 1995, at none other than Disney World's Pleasure Island—the same spot where Chris, Justin, and JC had run into Joey that one fateful night. Lou wanted the guys to perform in front of a young audience to capture what he hoped would be a vibrant reaction but also to get footage of NSYNC on tape that he could further use to shop the band around.

In order to get an audience into the venue, Justin's mom, Lynn, recalled to VH1 that she was able to get Disney to hand over all the fan mail that was once sent to Justin and JC while they were on *The All-New Mickey Mouse Club*. She grabbed all the addresses and mailed the households a flyer promoting the Pleasure Island show. The idea worked, and NSYNC was able to both pack the venue and, sure enough, elicit high-pitched screaming from the girls in the crowd. "Nobody knew who they were but it seemed like they had something going on," Joey's brother Steven recalled of that seminal early gig.

Johnny Wright, who was already working with Lou managing Backstreet Boys at the time, got hold of the Pleasure Island footage and NSYNC's short demo tape, and even though Lou had lied to him originally about working with NSYNC, Johnny was impressed with what he saw and heard and agreed to take on this boy band too.

By early 1996, he just so happened to be with the Backstreet Boys in Germany and had meetings with Jan Bolz, then president of BMG Music, who basically said "give me more" of that American boy band music. "He had said, 'I love all the American acts that you guys are bringing over to Germany now; if there's any more acts back in the US that you want me to take a look at, just let me know," Johnny told VH1. So, Johnny showed off an NSYNC promo photo and played the demo to Jan and his team and—unlike American music honchos—the Europeans were hooked. They wanted to fly to Orlando to see NSYNC for themselves, live and in person, and told Johnny, "If we like it, then we're going to sign them."

Johnny then arranged a meeting with the BMG executives, during which the members of NSYNC performed; it was also Johnny's first time meeting the five boy banders in person. Initially, the record label reps were intrigued ("my first impression was that they were working on a really high level and were really, really talented," Jan told VH1). But the team expressed some concerns about the band's kitschy name, not understanding what it meant and saying it was too hard to pronounce for non-English speakers, and with Lance, who didn't seem to be able to keep up with the choreography. Discussions came up about firing the bass singer, but the band refused, saying it was the five of them or nothing (and with Lance promising he would work double time to get up to speed). BMG conceded and decided to sign the band to their European imprint, BMG Ariola Munich, in the beginning of 1996.

Of course, that meant the boys (and Diane Bass and Lynn Harless) were packing up the

Orlando house and re-settling in Europe. And once again, they found themselves trying to hone in on their sound, which, in this case, also meant somehow appealing to throngs of non-English-speaking music fans. "All of the sudden, we get signed to Germany, and we have to start thinking about the European market—which, at that time, was a different sound than America had," Lance told *Billboard*, adding that BMG was the one to first pick NSYNC's songs and their producers. "If you listen to our first German album, there's a lot of songs on there that were not on the American version because we totally were like a techno band on some of those songs."

The guys also struggled a bit with the image that was being thrust upon them, one that they weren't sure really meshed with the more R&B, vocal-harmony music they wanted to create. "I think we could've been a lot better right out of the gate if [Lou] wasn't there trying to push us into this mold. The word boy band wasn't even out then, and it was almost like Lou knew what that was," Chris told *Huffington Post*. "So to be in this band where it was like, 'OK, we want you to dress as clowns. OK, now we want you to be in the swimming pool with your shirts off.' There were so many times where we thought why are we doing this? This is stupid."

Still, BMG moved ahead with the vision and lined up a crew of solid producers in Sweden who had also previously worked with the Backstreet Boys: Denniz Pop and Max Martin, the lauded duo behind Cheiron Studios. In fact, they were the masterminds of NSYNC's earliest hits, "I Want You Back" and "Tearin' Up My Heart."

The *New Yorker* calls Max nothing short of a "genius," "the Cyrano de Bergerac of today's pop landscape," and "music's magic melody

man," qualifying their assertion with the fact that the very accomplished songwriter has written 21 number-one hits in the pop milieu (not too far off from the Beatles masters Paul McCartney and John Lennon). Among his pop opuses are Katy Perry's "I Kissed A Girl," Britney Spears's ". . . Baby One More Time," and even a few for reigning queen Taylor Swift. It's a true feat considering that, born in 1971, Max was around the same age as Chris Kirkpatrick when he wound up working with NSYNC in Sweden.

Martin's mentor was Denniz Pop, who himself had been behind huge hits for Ace of Base and fellow Swede Robyn. And had Pop not sadly passed away in 1998 from cancer (the

Justin with Max Martin (left) and producer Karl Johan Schuster at the Academy Awards in 2017.

THINKING OF YOU, JOHNNY

Although many people have called themselves the "sixth member" of NSYNC (Jason Galasso, Shaq, and Lou among them), really that honorary distinction should go to manager Johnny Wright, who, along with his former wife Donna, has been more instrumental in the career of the boy band (and much of the '90s/'00s pop nebulous) than any other figure—including Lou Pearlman.

While Lou may have financed NSYNC and Backstreet Boys and became an infamous figurehead in the boy band scene, it was really his right-hand man Johnny Wright who made the big moves that turned both acts into household names. Johnny was the one who originally had the pivotal idea to first try launching the Backstreet Boys in Europe, and then followed the successful model with NSYNC. As the *St. Petersburg Times* has heralded him, he's the man who "helped shape a multibillion-dollar industry built for youths and their parents."

Epic Records exec David McPherson, who signed the Backstreet Boys to Jive Records, told the newspaper, "In '93, if groups sold a few records in Europe, so be it. But Johnny was ahead of his time on this, and it benefitted not only the Backstreet Boys but everything else that followed. . . . As far as I'm concerned, the Backstreet Boys set a tone for a whole new generation of music we now know as teen pop."

By all accounts, Johnny was destined to be a part of the boy band yearbook. His first taste of the music industry, in fact, was with Maurice Starr, the man behind New Edition and New Kids On The Block. Fresh out of college, Johnny was hosting a disco-themed segment on a radio station out of Cape Cod, Massachusetts, not far from Maurice's stomping grounds in Boston. Maurice noticed Johnny was slating in the mogul's records and extended an offer to the young host to invest in a national talent show he was hosting. That event ended up netting New Edition.

Though Johnny didn't have the money to invest at the time, Maurice didn't forget about him. He soon gave the DJ a job as the road manager for his new act, New Kids On The Block. That turned into a four-year-long stint in which he then became part of their management team.

After New Kids broke up, Maurice had Johnny working with his European act, Snap!, which was how he first got acquainted with international promotion. And after Johnny and his wife and kids relocated to Orlando, he continued his music ventures after taking a meeting with Lou Pearlman, who entrusted Johnny first with Backstreet and then NSYNC. Backstreet wasn't too keen on the idea of sharing, though, and gave Johnny his walking papers when the other Orlando boy band came along. With his full attention on NSYNC, Johnny propelled them into the limelight, including nabbing an all-too-important Disney special in 1998 (ironically, one that Backstreet passed on).

Soon enough, Johnny also became the manager of Britney Spears, the Jonas Brothers, Janet Jackson, and even a new version of Menudo. Today, Johnny is behind the Wright Entertainment Group, which manages 98 Degrees as well as the solo careers of AJ McLean and Justin Timberlake.

Of working with NSYNC, Johnny told the *St. Petersburg Times*, "I don't care if 'N Sync never would have had the success they did. I enjoyed being with them. That's what it was all about. We just got blessed to be where we are right now."

same year Backstreet Boys dedicated the video for their song, "Show Me the Meaning of Being Lonely," to him), he no doubt would've gone on to earn just as much acclaim as Martin.

What the production duo did with Backstreet Boys and NSYNC that was brilliant was follow a formula that the Swedes had long established—and it worked. The "songs use major and minor chords in surprising combinations (going to a minor chord on the chorus, say, when you least expect it), producing happy songs that sound sad, and sad songs that make you happy—tunes that serve a wide variety of moods," explains the *New Yorker*. Max and Denniz's handiwork in crafting the early sound of NSYNC, and really all of mid-'90s pop, cannot be understated.

As it was, other than Chris, who had written original songs that he performed in and around Orlando before NSYNC got off the ground, the other guys really didn't have a ton of experience penning music. Justin and JC had just started working on material together after the demise of *The All-New Mickey Mouse Club* in 1994 when they got the call from Chris about joining his pop band, and Joey and Lance were new to the game.

Yet joining forces with Max and Denniz, whom the guys have often described as looking like Vikings with a constant chain of cigarettes hanging out of their mouths, "It was the first time that we got to work with huge producers that had hits on the radio. And they made us feel so comfortable, and we just had so much fun," Lance told *Billboard*. Hearing what they did with Robyn boosted their morale, Lance added. "We loved that sound that Robyn had. . . . It was more pop than we were used to, but we got to use our R&B vocals with these pop tracks. It was the perfect combination." It was the exact bridge the band needed to cross the tired R&B a cappella style they had been working on with a fresher, more relevant sound.

Still, it took a lot of hard work to get there. "I just remember always being so tired in the studio," said Lance. "Any free time went into three things: sleep, to catch up with somebody back home, or find out what are we doing next," JC added. "Our schedule was pretty busy, so there wasn't a lot of wasted time. For a few years of our lives, literally every hour was accounted for."

In those foundational sessions, the groundwork was also laid out for how the five-part vocal arrangements would ensue, thereby creating the framework for NSYNC in the years ahead. Two guys stood out right away for having the strongest voices: Justin and JC. "[They] had by far the best lead voices. It was a matter of which one of them was singing what part," Chris told *Billboard*. "And then, if there were a lot of harmonies, they'd throw me on. I had a really high falsetto, and a really, really high voice, so I could layer and do doubles and octaves, and do octaves of octaves. We almost countrified out some of the songs by putting so many harmonies on everything we did."

None of the guys took it personally either. As Joey told the magazine, there was no animosity—ever. "There was no, 'Oh my god, he's singing more leads than I am.' Guess what? We all get the same fucking paycheck. It didn't matter. . . . We loved [the music], and we still do."

The first single NSYNC put out, with the help of Max and Denniz, was the Euro electro dance hit, "I Want You Back." It was released on October 7, 1996 (nearly one year to the day after their inaugural Pleasure Island gig). By November 18, a month and a half later, it was

Deniz Pop in 1994.

fan magazines, as well as a relentless stream of early tour dates across thirty-plus international markets, NSYNC became a frenzy, often recognized and mobbed in the streets.

"It was crazy because we would have thousands of fans chasing us down the street and we'd be on the cover of every magazine," Lance told *Entertainment Weekly.* But it came at a price, with the guys never getting time off to rest and relax. "They were so serious about their job and what they were doing, that they didn't care if it killed them," Justin's mom, Lynn, told VH1. But being the protective parent she was, Lynn called the record company and demanded the boys get one day off each and every week.

Yet not one member of NSYNC would take back any of those moments. "From the inside, the early German record was a period of growth," JC told *People* of the two-year span NSYNC spent in Europe. During that time, they got to know themselves and who they were as musicians, so that by the time they came back home to America, they were more confident pop stars ready for the next phase. "We were experiencing so many new things for the first time. With those experiences under our belt, by the time we were shifting focus back to the US releases, we had begun evolving into our next expressions," he added. "Every project seems to take on new life, and the fact that the shift to the US felt like a new project even though there was some carryover, we were already naturally shifting into another era and mode."

already a huge hit, landing in a Top 10 spot on the German music charts. They filmed a video for the song that "looked like it cost $5 to make," recalled JC—though the band would eventually redo the visual accompaniment for the American market (i.e. MTV) upon getting their US deal in early 1998.

"Tearin' Up My Heart" came next, on February 10, 1997, still relegated to Germany and European territories. Another single, "Here We Go," came on May 5, 1997, and then three weeks later, the original European version of the band's self-titled debut was released via Trans Continental and BMG, to much fanfare. By its second week on the streets, it hit the No. 1 spot on the German charts.

Nearly overnight, the band became a huge success. As mom, Lynn, recalls, Justin got a gold record for "I Want You Back" and turned 16 on the same day in early 1997. Through promotional appearances on European talk shows and radio and features in teen-oriented

In Sync with NSYNC

'90s boy band fans were competitive. You were either on Team BSB or Team NSYNC. I followed all the boy bands—from the UK's Boyzone and Take That to Orlando's finest, the Backstreet Boys. They won my heart from the first moment I heard "Quit Playing Games," but when NSYNC burst onto the scene with "I Want You Back," we all knew there was going to be some serious rivalry. I couldn't deny this group had catchy songs too. Soon, I had their album and went to see them in concert (fun fact: Britney Spears was their opening act!). Around that time, I was hired as a high school reporter for *Teen People*'s news team and got to cover NSYNC performing live outside Macy's Herald Square in New York City. My best friend and I watched

from the front row and got passes to meet the guys after the show. I had no idea the impact that NSYNC—especially Justin Timberlake—would have on the world, or how my love of boy bands would inspire my life. These days, I'm a mom of two and proudly brag to my kids as they watch the *Trolls* movie series—particularly *Trolls Band Together,* during which NSYNC reunited—that I grew up having adventures with my friends as we followed this group. My son sings along to NSYNC songs and told me his teacher played "Bye Bye Bye" at the end of the day. It makes me proud. Listening to these hits now is really special, not only because it brings back so many memories, but also because it reminds us of who we were back in the day—before marriage, children, and juggling careers. Each time I listen to an NSYNC song, I reconnect to my hopes and dreams.

Joelle Speranza, author of *The Comeback Tour*, a romance novel that pays tribute to boy bands

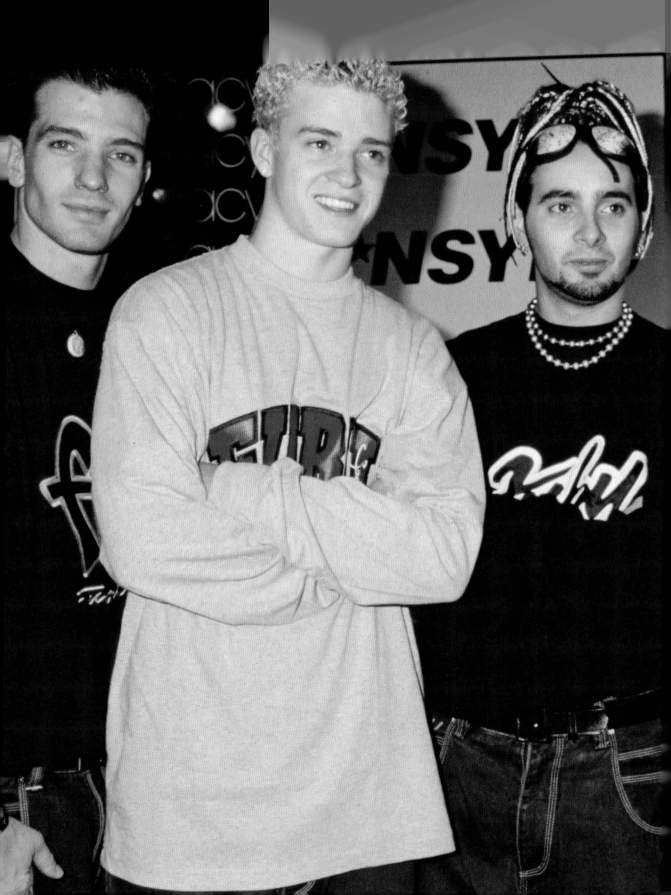

The guys at Macy's
Back-To-School
Celebration in
New York City
in August 1998.

COMING HOME TO AMERICA

"If we didn't break the States, we weren't gonna break. I was real nervous about how it was gonna be perceived by everybody. . . . We'd do a show over in Europe in front of 8 to 10 million people that was the biggest show over there, then we'd come over here, and our parents would forget to pick us up from the airport."

—Chris talking to *Billboard* in 2018

In 1997, NSYNC embarked on the For The Girl Tour around Europe. Taking its name from the song "For The Girl Who Has Everything," off their self-titled debut album, the tour was a mix of nightclub and concert-hall gigs as well as state fairs and radio music fests, with the shows getting bigger as the band's profile grew. There was even a big, multi-band radio bash in Dortmund, Germany, in February 1997, headlined by the Backstreet Boys and featuring the Spice Girls. NSYNC was fourteenth in the band order. The two boy bands met again several months later at the Pepsi Pop Fest '97 in Rotterdam, Netherlands, where Backstreet Boys and Aaron Carter headlined and NSYNC was at the bottom of the band order list. This discrepancy gave further credence to the supposedly percolating boy band rivalry.

To assuage the tensions and create a copacetic environment for fans, Backstreet and NSYNC competed in a fun, sold-out basketball game that year for 10,000 European attendees. "We thought if we put a game together, the fans would see that there was no rivalry between each other but that

NSYNC with their Bambi Award (one of Germany's biggest media awards) in 1997.

The Spice Girls in 1997.

they were friends," dual band manager Johnny Wright explained to VH1. In the end, NSYNC lost the game by one point.

"There were a lot of times kids would come to our shows and say things like, 'I'm only here because the Backstreet Boys aren't here,'" Chris recalled to *People*. "That happened to us all the time! . . . The crazy thing is, they all said it. You're talking about a time way, way, way back where we were trying to promote our first single, and it was crazy because it was obvious. There was no point that we'd get mad about that because we know that the majority of the kids were coming to our shows because they were Backstreet Boys fans and they wanted to see what this was like."

But once NSYNC's debut album went to the No. 1 spot on the German charts a week after its late May release in 1997, that all changed. Beyond Germany, fans in Switzerland and Austria caught on, as did most of Eastern Europe, where more than 800,000 copies of the album sold. The band put out two more singles—"For The Girl Who Has Everything" in August 1997 and "Together Again" in November 1997—that further spread the word about the popular act and solidified a very successful year for the quintet overseas.

One of the people who caught word was Vince DeGiorgio, who, at the time, was under the BMG umbrella in New York City, helming the label's subsidiary division, RCA Records. Vince's job was basically the reverse of Jan Bolz's—"I went out to find international repertoire that we thought would be great for the United States market," he told

VH1's *Driven*. There was a huge sea change in radio in late '97. Hanson's "MmmBop," Spice Girls' "Wannabe," and Backstreet Boys' "Quit Playing Games (With My Heart)" were in the top 15 spots on the *Billboard* charts over the course of the year, while other R&B influences also reigned supreme (as evidenced by top placements by Monica, Toni Braxton, R. Kelly, Usher, and Keith Sweat).

By this time, grunge had largely been phased out and pop was becoming more and more of a presence in the market. Johnny knew this and had the great foresight to keep promoting Backstreet and NSYNC in his music circles. As the *St. Petersburg Times* recalled, "He knew that New Kids had hit big in the era of Mötley Crüe, tattoos and drugs, and he sensed that parents were crying out for a change in what their children listened to" in the late '90s too.

Vince DeGiorgio happened to be in attendance at NSYNC's show in Budapest, Hungary, in November 1997, and he was hooked. "I just saw something I hadn't seen in a lot of people; they were completely confident, they were completely on a mission," Vince shared with VH1. He had to have them on his roster. "I was so impressed with the show I said, 'Okay, you guys did your job and I'm gonna go back and do mine.'" Vince insisted to RCA that NSYNC must be signed—and he had his way before the holidays came around in 1997. It was just the right time, since "the boys were ready to come home," Karen Chasez said in *Driven*.

After two very productive years in Europe, it was finally time for NSYNC to head back Stateside and make their impression on an American audience. RCA opted to run with the music the boys had already developed with

Max and Denniz (since the songs had caused such a frenzy overseas). The label started by re-releasing the song, "I Want You Back," as the first single in America on January 20, 1998. But the climb to the top of the charts was slow.

"They got off the plane [in the US] and nobody was cheering. You heard crickets," Joe Fatone Sr. recalled to VH1. Son Steven added, "The [guys] were like, 'Hey we're huge.' And we're like, 'America doesn't know who you guys are.'"

Joey's current manager, Joe Mulvihill, also recalled the great homecoming at the Orlando airport to *People*. "His mom and I went down to the gate and we had a sign, 'Welcome home'—it was just us two. And Joey came out of the plane in this big puffer jacket that had the *NSYNC logo. And he was like, 'Oh, it's so nice to have nobody bothering me.' . . . We thought he was making it up, until one day he showed me a VHS tape . . . and my jaw hit the floor. And then I turned ultra-proud, like, 'Dude, are you serious? Is this really happening?'"

Other than Justin's and Lance's moms, who had been with their young sons during their international spell, the other families had no idea the amount of success the boys had overseas. There was no social media, YouTube, TikTok, et al., in 1998, so the way that import/export acts can migrate to new territories today with the click of a button on a computer or smartphone was not an available mechanism in that time. And unless you were there witnessing the fandemonium, it was hard to understand the magnitude. Thankfully, Joey and his obsession with filming everything came in handy at this point.

"Joey would give us VHS tapes . . . friends would be around and you'd pop in this tape. You're looking at their faces and suddenly they see this idiot who's been their friend forever, no big deal, walk out in front of tens of thousands of kids just losing their minds, throwing stuffed animals and shirts. And they'd see that and their mouths would just drop," Chris told *People.* "And we're like, 'See, this is what we've been dealing with.'"

Although it was quite the shell shock to come home and have their anonymity intact again, Justin, JC, Joey, Chris, and Lance stuck with the project—and so did RCA. "They were willing to go right back at the bottom and work their way back up to the top," Johnny recalled about the band's humbling moment. And even though the first US single, "I Want You Back," was severely underperforming in the States, BMG/RCA went forward with re-releasing NSYNC's self-titled debut album a couple months later, on March 24, 1998—albeit with some changes that were more attuned to the American market.

Several tracks that appeared on the original German release were nixed altogether, including "Best Of My Life," "Riddle," "Together Again," "More Than A Feeling," and "Forever Young." The RCA team also lined up remixes of "I Want You Back," "For The Girl Who Has Everything," and "Tearin' Up My Heart" for the American release. There were also four additional songs added that were exclusive to the US version of *NSYNC*—that list included one of their eventual big hits, "Thinking of You (I Drive Myself Crazy)," as well as "I Just Wanna Be With You," "(God Must Have Spent) A Little More Time On You," and "Everything I Own," a cover of a Bread song. On most of the songs, Justin and JC shared lead vocal duty, but Chris had a good spotlight on "Thinking of You (I Drive Myself Crazy)," as did Joey and Chris on "Together Again."

For the new tracks, the RCA team enlisted songwriters like Rick Nowels and Ellen Shipley (who had worked with Kim Wilde and Belinda Carlisle), and Carl Sturken and Evan Rogers (who worked with Christina Aguilera and would become instrumental in the career of Rihanna), as well as the hip-hop/R&B group Full Force. "There were some great cuts on there [the original record], but they did need some additional things to really blend in to what was going on over here [in America]," Carl Sturken told VH1.

A new music video was filmed for "I Want You Back" that updated the shoddy, cheap, green-screen iteration NSYNC originally filmed in Germany. The new video upgraded the laughable spaceship-esque exploration in the former to a more active, realistic scenario that showed the guys driving around picking up girls, playing hoops and pool, and jet skiing— and also had tons of close-ups, especially of baby-face Justin with his new hoop earring.

NSYNC also made music videos for the US release of "Thinking Of You (I Drive Myself Crazy)," complete with the padded-wall room and straightjackets, which hasn't exactly aged well. There were also videos for "Here We Go" with a basketball game and pep rally motif; the retro-tinged "(God Must Have Spent) A Little More Time On You" with mother-and-son tearjerker moments; and the photo-shoot-themed/dance-routine-heavy "Tearin' Up My Heart." Additional videos were made for international territories, including "U Drive Me Crazy" (a UK exclusive), "For The Girl Who Has Everything," and "Together Again."

Even so, the album had a dismal US debut. A couple weeks after its release on March 24, 1998, *NSYNC* made its entrance on the *Billboard* Top 200 chart on April 11—at No. 82. At the

WHAT THE CRITICS SAID

The members of NSYNC have had their own personal opinions about the various singles and tracks on their self-titled debut. According to interviews with *Billboard*, "Tearin' Up My Heart" was Lance's favorite (he deemed it as "'I Want You Back' on crack"), while he said the "too cheesy" track "Here We Go" was the "bane of my existence." And JC liked the version of "I Want You Back" re-done for the US album, as he believed it had more "pace" and "energy" than the original.

But how did critics respond? Like with most boy bands of the era, critical reactions were mixed.

"A quintet of freshly scrubbed young men whose music—surprise—is not only infectious but crisply executed and downright ambitious at times . . . it would be hasty to dismiss the group as a mere flavor of the month."

—Chuck Taylor, *Billboard*

"A pleasing piece of ear candy . . . *NSYNC don't have the charisma or tunes of the Spice Girls or All Saints on this debut . . . The only thing the five boys of *NSYNC have is good looks, good producers, and a couple of catchy singles like 'I Want You Back.' That's enough for a hit, and not quite enough for an album. Even so, the filler is well made and competently performed, which means their teen fans will enjoy the album while it's hot."

—Stephen Thomas Erlewine, *AllMusic*

"When it comes to the meat and potato of this self-titled LP, there is little to hold interest past that single ['Tearin' Up My Heart']. The soft signature pop sound of the '90s is here, 'I Just Wanna Be With You' and '(God Must Have Spent) A Little More Time On You' have that slick Michael Jackson production, coupled together well with the group's soothing vocal work, which perks up interest somewhat and is catchy and enjoyable to listen to, but the level of quality isn't the same, and for the most part tracks are fairly dull."

—Simon K, *Sputnikmusic*

The group is interviewed in Germany in 1997.

time, the number one album was the *Titanic* soundtrack, with other spots in the Top 10 filled by Madonna, Usher, Savage Garden, Eric Clapton, and, yes, the Backstreet Boys (who were holding strong at No. 6). NSYNC's debut sold only 14,000 units. It was a shock, to say the least, to the band and their team. "We were a little discouraged, thinking, 'Well, I guess we'll never be able to create that craziness we had in Europe. We'll just have a normal career here,'" Lance told *Huffington Post*.

While NSYNC's songs were on the radio (not only "I Want You Back" but also "Tearin' Up My Heart," which was released as a second single on June 30, 1998), there was no "face of the music," Johnny recalled to VH1. And so they started taking whatever gigs they could in America, including in the parking lot of the Florida Walmart where Chris's mom worked. While they were not sure what the reception would be, a sizable crowd of 2,000 people showed up.

The band started gaining steam, particularly in their hometown in Orlando, and by May 2, "I Want You Back" was also charting on *Billboard*'s Hot 100 chart, peaking at No. 13. ("Tearin' Up My Heart" wouldn't do as well, however, only peaking at No. 59.) Joey recalled to *Billboard* he first heard "I Want You Back" on the radio in a spot featured on Orlando station XL 106.7. It was chosen for a listening battle in which the song was pitted up against another track from another new band and listeners would call in to vote for their favorites. "And all of a sudden it was like *NSYNC, *NSYNC, *NSYNC—we won every day or every week for a bunch of weeks," he said.

The real game-changing moment, however, came in the summer of 1998, when Disney once again proved to be an important ally and booked NSYNC for a special concert for the Disney Channel. In fact, in a weird twist of fate, it was originally the Backstreet Boys that Disney had lined up, but that five-piece ultimately declined the offer. Some have said it was due to a heavy plate of prior obligations, though Joey told *Billboard* it was because BSB member Brian Littrell needed heart surgery. When BSB pulled out, though, Johnny Wright had just the right pick to replace them—his other band, NSYNC. His push was helped by a phone call from the band's RCA publicist, Elaine Shock, who pitched NSYNC's potential, harping on the fact that they had blown up overseas.

After listening to the music and pouring through promo photos, Disney was in. The guys had three weeks to prepare for the concert filming, which wasn't a lot of time to put together a full headlining show, especially when the guys had mostly performed shorter radio fest appearances in Europe up to that point. But, according to longtime choreographer Darrin Henson, the five worked their butts off to prepare and were ready for the gig, which was filmed at Walt Disney World in Orlando in late May in front of the Mann Chinese Theater at MGM Studios (today, Hollywood Studios). *People* has called it "the most important gig during *NSYNC's seven-year run."

Disney and team NSYNC saw something curious happen as the family network ran three weeks of promos leading up to the main event—every time a promo aired, there was a boost in sales of the self-titled debut record. It was also just the boost of morale the guys needed to get the concert special just right.

As RCA head Vince attested, "everything came together that night" for the Disney show. The guys were in top form, performing numbers like "I Want You Back," "Crazy for You," "I Just Wanna Be with You," and "(God Must Have Spent) A Little More Time on You." The crowd was massive and shrieked

between numbers. "They pulled it off, they won the hearts of every American who saw it," choreographer Darrin remembered.

After the *Disney: In Concert* special finally aired on July 18, 1998 (and kept airing in copious reruns on the Disney Channel), NSYNC's album had sold 500,000 copies. "I didn't know they were going to air it like three times a day for four months. Once it started airing, that's when the tides started changing—one morning we woke up, and everyone knew our name," Lance told *Billboard*.

By October 10 of that year, the debut album shot up to the No. 2 spot on the *Billboard* 200 chart and stayed on the chart for 109 weeks total, including 30 weeks within the Top 10.

After the first two singles, "I Want You Back" and "Tearin' Up My Heart" in 1998, two more singles from *NSYNC* followed. On February 9, 1999, came "(God Must Have Spent) A Little More Time on You" (which hit No. 8 on the *Billboard* Hot 100 chart); Alabama's cover of the song also netted a Grammy nomination in 1999 for "Best Country Collaboration with Vocals." Also in February came "Thinking of You (I Drive Myself Crazy)." Initially, it didn't track on the *Billboard* charts, but it was a *TRL* mainstay, remaining at No. 1 for 40 days.

The *NSYNC* album ultimately ended up selling 10 million copies in the US, with the Recording Industry Association of America® certifying it 10× Platinum and presenting the guys with a diamond award. In 1998 alone came 4.4 million sold copies, making *NSYNC* the fifth best-selling record of the year in the US, per Nielsen SoundScan (now Luminate) data. And, across the globe, the album has sold more than 15 million copies to date. Things were changing at rapid pace for the group in 1998. It was the dawn of NSYNC hysteria.

JC, Justin, Chris, Joey, and Lance perform at Macy's Herald Square in New York for their August 1998 Back-To-School Celebration.

IN SYNC WITH POP CULTURE

The [fans have] followed everything you've done and love everything you do and everything about you. . . . They talk to you like they actually knew you, even though you've never met these people before in your life. . . It's a weird, surreal feeling. Even to this day, I've never gotten used to it."

—Joey talking to *Huffington Post* in 2018

After the *Disney: In Concert* special made them overnight sensations, Justin, JC, Joey, Chris, and Lance were *everywhere* in the late '90s and early '00s. Whether their smiling visages were on scores of memorabilia or basically any TV channel you could flip to, NSYNC took the culture crown around the dawn of the new millennium. As the *Los Angeles Times* exclaimed, they were a "musical, economic, and hormonal powerhouse."

Unlike the rebuffed reactions NSYNC got from American music honchos in 1995 before they went abroad to kick off their career in Europe, offers were now rolling in for appearances, merch, and tour dates—and the guys and their team jumped on most of them. When the members of NSYNC weren't in full glossy display on covers and in centerfolds of teeny bopper magazines like *Tiger Beat* and respected music bibles like *Rolling Stone*, they appeared on talk shows from *Live With Regis and Kathie Lee* to *The Rosie O'Donnell Show*. They even had a cameo on *Sesame Street*.

But it was MTV's *Total Request Live* that became a turning point. As mentioned in the last chapter, "Thinking of You (I Drive Myself Crazy)" broke a record for *TRL*, remaining in the No. 1 spot for

A promo photo of NSYNC in Germany in 1999.

40 days on the network. Due to the intense demand, the *Los Angeles Times* recalled, "MTV . . . has responded by devoting entire weekends of programming to [NSYNC]."

When the guys appeared in the window-filled *TRL* studio, where someone at street level could get a glimpse of the fab five, it was pandemonium. Fans lined up all around Times Square in a modern-day display of "Beatlemania." As host of MTV's *TRL* Carson Daly said when feting NSYNC at their Hollywood Walk of Fame Star ceremony, "I was one of the very lucky people who got to hang with these guys when the entire world wanted to hang with them."

Part of the appeal was tied to the all-important teen and preteen demographic, the same audience that sent New Edition, New Kids On The Block, Backstreet Boys, and the like skyrocketing. It was a curious time in 1998—as discussed in this book, the dominating grunge music scene in the early and mid-'90s had come to an impasse, with a huge cloud hanging over the scene after the death of Nirvana's Kurt Cobain in 1994. And as bands like BSB, Hanson, and the Spice Girls came to market, pop music started gaining steam again with the youngest consumers.

"Two-and-a-half years ago, we were at the tail end of the grunge era," Mercury Records A&R Steven Greenberg (the man behind Hanson) told *Rolling Stone* in 1998. "And everyone doubted that a pure pop act could get on the radio. People forgot that most of the kids in America aren't particularly unhappy and would relate to music that said life can be good. Everyone was aiming at an audience college age and above and hoping that the music would trickle down. The younger audience had no choice but to listen to music that was created for a much older audience, while today there's music being created for a younger audience."

Justin on the cover of *Tiger Beat* in 2003.

And that younger audience devoured pop music whole. *Rolling Stone* pointed to staggering figures, noting that, in 1998, teen-oriented pop music was 10 percent of total record sales. In fact, the magazine said, high schoolers ponied up $2.7 billion on records, concert tickets, merch, and anything else band-related that they could get their hands on. The lucrative community was a real tipping point for marketers since there were "31 million teenagers in America, with an estimated $122 billion in disposable income." Knowing NSYNC's pull, it was a huge opportunity for many to bank off their image, especially if teenagers got to see them up close.

Even before the *Disney: In Concert* special aired ad nauseum in July 1998, NSYNC had packed their bags and set off on their first American tour. NSYNC In Concert kicked off June 11, 1998, and ran through September 23 of that year. The band initially played to smaller concert halls (a number of House of Blues venues were on the inaugural run of dates). But by the time the tour was extended and rebranded to the Second II None Tour in November of that year, something had changed.

In the middle of NSYNC's headline 1998–99 tour came one of their first big industry breaks, when the band was tapped to open ten dates of the second North American leg of Janet Jackson's Velvet Rope Tour in 1998. Beginning October 14 in Baltimore and running through October 31 in Houston, the short list of shows were some of NSYNC's first major public appearances. Massive stadiums brought NSYNC into the purview of millions of people. In fact, the guys—who were all fans of the megastar—had seen the concert at the Orlando Arena when the tour first kicked off, before they were asked to join it. "I just want to say about two to three years ago I had her poster on my wall, so I'm psyched," Justin told MTV about getting hyped for NSYNC's slot on the tour.

By just the third date, at a show in Auburn Hills, Michigan (just outside of Detroit), Lance said there was a tangible turning point for the band—the moment he knew NSYNC had made it. "I've never heard a noise like that before," he told *BuzzFeed News* of the pivotal gig where crowds were cheering for the boy band. "You get these goose bumps and they don't go away the whole time you're onstage."

The guys didn't actually get paid for the gig, according to manager Johnny Wright, who recalls getting a call from a talent agent saying Janet was personally looking for new acts to take on the road with her for a string of dates, but there would be no money involved. Even so, the exposure was priceless and Johnny knew it when he accepted the offer on the band's

behalf. Plus, the hands-on experience was invaluable, too, as Lance has said, "We got to learn how a tour really works. Janet was a huge inspiration for our future stage shows."

For the occasion, the guys wore capes and Daft Punk-looking space suits with helmets, most of which they tore off early into the set, which certainly grabbed people's attention. "The performance got a better response than Janet Jackson did," Justin and Lance's early vocal coach Bob Westbrook told VH1's *Driven*. "I said, 'You watch, these guys will be bigger than the Beatles.'"

And for a time, they kind of were. By the time Janet's tour wrapped and NSYNC went back out on the road for their own rebranded tour, they were playing enormous venues themselves, including Madison Square Garden in New York City as part of Jingle Ball, and the San Jose Arena.

Their first tour had four iterations total, later rebranded once again to the Ain't No Stoppin' Us Now Tour (March–June 1999) and the Boys of Summer Tour (July–September 1999), with some "Winter Shows" added as makeup dates during the 1999 holiday season. In total, the road jaunt ran for 18 months, visiting 100-plus cities for some 200 shows. To open the dates, NSYNC had a sizable list of rotating acts that included Britney Spears, Mandy Moore, and even New Kids On The Block member Jordan Knight, who had by then embarked on a solo career.

The tour did so well it was nominated in the category of Best New Artist Tour by prestigious industry magazine *Pollstar*. And by the time all was said and done, NSYNC's concerts were the third-highest-grossing of 1999, just behind the Rolling Stones and Bruce Springsteen, with more than $51 million

in ticket sales. The production had major sponsors, too, like teen zit cream brand Oxy Balance and Clairol Herbal Essences hair care. "NSYNC Day" was proclaimed by a radio station in Connecticut. And the concerts got overwhelming praise too.

London Free Press exclaimed of an Ontario date, "It was the up-tempo material that drew the best response, as the members bounced around the stage in tightly choreographed dance routines, proving that they can dance too . . . And there was no question they knew exactly how to play the crowd, providing just enough pelvic thrusts amid the earnest and squeaky-clean production."

Music Express tipped their hat after an Edmonton show, remarking, "Say what you want about boy-groups with millions of dollars in production at their disposal. They may be pinnacle of pop fluff, but they're not putting on boring concerts."

And a Los Angeles Times review in 1999 called the concert "a high-energy explosion of music and dancing that includes towers of flame, a cheesy space monster . . . videos, and more than a half-dozen costume changes. . . . The show, of course, is a huge hit with the fans. The dance numbers, solos and stage antics emphasize each member's well-defined personality—the cute one, the serious one,

NSYNC celebrates with a special plaque for one million record sales, backstage at their Ain't No Stoppin' Us Now Tour in April 1999.

POP KING AND QUEEN

Romantic liaisons have notoriously been frowned upon in the boy band world—to at least try to keep the illusion that the guys are all available and just waiting to meet the fangirl of their dreams. "I'm twenty-seven years old; I'm allowed to date!" Chris once pleaded with *Rolling Stone* readers.

But, sometimes, there are those relationships too good not to capture public interest and become tabloid fodder. Enter Justin and Britney. The relationship between the reigning pop king and queen of the late 90s/early 2000s was a slow launch at first. The two met when they were eleven-year-old cohorts on *The All-New Mickey Mouse Club*. Britney revealed that, during this innocent time, Justin locked lips with her during a game of "Truth Or Dare," her first kiss. Justin also thought of that early time fondly, once telling *GQ*, "I was infatuated with her from the moment I saw her."

Though some time passed, the two reconnected in late 1998, when Britney opened for NSYNC on their Second II None Tour, and she and Justin began dating in 1999. At the time, NSYNC was riding a career high and Britney was just getting started, as her . . . *Baby One More Time* debut album readied for launch.

The two attempted to deny their relationship at first, including in the press, but they softly confirmed it by sitting together at the 2000 MTV VMAs (pictured on the next page) and then made it red carpet official at the 2001 American Music Awards, when they rolled out their infamous denim on denim on denim matching outfits (pictured at right). Justin even addressed the coupling on the otherwise high-brow CNN program *Larry King Live*, telling the host when pressed about the relationship, "Yes, she's a wonderful, wonderful person, and I'm very lucky, you know, to have somebody on the other side of the spectrum who understands all these things that I go through."

The three-year relationship became the epitome of pop culture front-page news until the couple's gobsmacker of a breakup in 2002, when accusations started flying. Britney has alleged Justin used the publicity to help propel his solo career ahead of his *Justified* album debut; Justin alluded to being cheated

...on by the pop star in his "Cry Me a River" video. This war of words continued for the next decade in various interviews by both parties.

In 2021, Justin issued an apology to Britney and Janet Jackson on social media for his part in the fallouts that befell both women after the respective relationship breakup and Super Bowl fracas (more on that on page 147). "I specifically want to apologize to Britney Spears and Janet Jackson both individually, because I care for and respect these women and I know I failed. . . . I also feel compelled to respond, in part, because everyone involved deserves better and most importantly, because this is a larger conversation that I wholeheartedly want to be a part of and grow from," Justin wrote.

In October 2023, Britney released her much-talked-about memoir, *The Woman In Me*, shedding more light on her side of the story, including claims that she was pressured to have an abortion after getting pregnant with Justin's baby; that he provided the media with a narrative of her promiscuity after their breakup in order to remain the good guy; that he was actually the one who cheated on her countless times (negating the "Cry Me a River" video hypothesis); and that he eventually broke up with Brit via text message.

The fallout was palpable. Justin took a brief break from social media, with reps saying he wanted to "focus on his own family" and "grow and evolve instead of bringing up the past." And his bandmates came to his defense, asking to "practice a little forgiveness." But, according to *Page Six*, he was "concerned" and rightfully so, as he has been dogged by Britney fans ever since.

When he released his new single, "Selfish," in January 2024 (oddly the same name as a track Britney released thirteen years prior), Brit's fans ensured he couldn't get to the top, instead spinning and re-spinning her song so it took the top of the iTunes charts. And when Justin appeared as the music guest on *Saturday Night Live* a few weeks later that January, *The Atlantic* went so far as to call it an "act of desperation" on Justin's part. "The tide has turned on Timberlake. . . . In the midst of trying to reboot his pop-music career . . . his persona has also undergone a cultural reckoning, especially in light of the revelations about him found in his ex Britney Spears's memoir," begins the article. "Timberlake has become emblematic of a casual mid-2000s white-male cockiness that doesn't play as well in 2024."

As of early 2024, Britney's book has sold 2 million copies, showing that interest in the pop star—and in the ultimate pop duo—has never truly waned.

A *TRL* photoshoot in 2000, feature NSYNC (to the right of the photo), as well as other stars of the time like Destiny's Child (bottom left), Britney Spears (bottom center), and Christina Aguilera (bottom right).

etc.—and it strikes powerful chords with the devoted fans."

Did they ever. A *Rolling Stone* profile in November 1998 describes the swarms of fangirls who found out where Joey lived in Orlando and followed him around, and the fact that Justin had just purchased a new Mercedes. The article also talked about the fan mail the guys would get on the daily, to the tune of 1,500 letters (which Joey's parents had the job of filtering through). Around the time the magazine's article went to press, NSYNC was prepping for an appearance at the 72nd annual Macy's Thanksgiving Day Parade, in which they appeared on the M&M'S float and offered a televised performance of "Tearin' Up My Heart."

They had also just released their one and only Christmas album (stealing a page out of the boy band playbook to put out holiday tunes when the popularity iron struck). Called *Home For Christmas*, NSYNC's seasonal record was released via Trans Continental and BMG/RCA on November 10, 1998, just a half year past the American launch of their self-titled debut.

Based on their growing star power, it's no surprise the album sold well—by October 1999, it had sold 2 million copies and was declared double Platinum by the Recording Industry Association of America®. Nielsen SoundScan data has ranked the album the fifteenth best-selling holiday record in the US. Upon its release, it also shot up to No. 7 on the

Billboard 200 chart and entered at No. 5 on the *Billboard Top Holiday Albums Chart*, meaning the boy band had two concurrent albums in the Top 10.

It was beloved by fans and the band alike. Lance even once admitted to *Billboard*, "By far, the Christmas album is my favorite album we've ever done," adding that the beautiful a cappella harmonies on "O Holy Night" took him back to "when we all got together in 1995."

The 14 tracks featured a mix of originals and covers, starting off with the first single, "Merry Christmas, Happy Holidays," an original tune co-written by Justin and JC alongside early producer Veit Renn. A music video was shot for the song, in which NSYNC takes over for a sick Santa and *Diff'rent Strokes* actor Gary Coleman plays an elf (a casting request that came from the band themselves). The video was shot in one day, due to NSYNC's in-demand schedule and in order to make it in time for MTV's holiday rotation. What director Lionel C. Martin remembered most about the shoot was that Justin was the guy "who had the most fun," as he told *Bustle* in honor of the song's twentieth anniversary in 2018.

Returning *NSYNC* songwriters Carl Sturken and Evan Rogers helped pen "I Never Knew the Meaning of Christmas." There were also Christmas standards, like the aforementioned "O Holy Night" and "The First Noel." The other special thing about this record is that—although Justin and JC continued to take on vocal leads on most tracks—Chris, Joey, and Lance get their turn in the spotlight on songs like "Under The Tree," "All I Want Is You (This Christmas)," and "The Only Gift."

The album received polarized reactions from critics. *Entertainment Weekly*'s Chris Willman panned it with an average "C" rating, noting, "Their writing stable simply strings together sentimental-sounding non sequiturs, an hour-

A celebratory cake backstage at an LA NSYNC concert at the Forum in April 1999.

The boys rehearse for the 1999 MTV Video Music Awards.

plus of which ultimately renders their initially alluring, smooth-as-a-baby's-bottom harmonies vaguely robotic." But *Bustle* has heralded it as "one of the best pop holiday records of all time," adding, "The 'O Holy Night' a capella shows off the group's killer harmonies, 'Kiss Me at Midnight' is the New Year's bop we'd been missing, and who could forget Lance's epic bass note in 'The Only Gift'?"

Over the span of 1998–1999, the gifts kept on coming. NSYNC also appeared as

themselves in an episode of *Sabrina The Teenage Witch*, popped up at the '99 MTV Video Music Awards (for which they also filmed a skit mocking the big blockbuster hit *Armageddon*), performed "I Want You Back" at the 1998 telecast of *Miss Teen USA*, and had appeared on several movie soundtracks, including *Pokémon: The First Movie* (contributing the song "Somewhere, Someday"); *Tarzan*, for which they recorded the song "Trashin' The Camp" with Phil Collins;

and Gloria Estefan's *Music of the Heart,* working with her for the movie's title track. "Music of My Heart" became a huge hit for both acts and was nominated for a Grammy in 1999 for Best Pop Collaboration with Vocals (though it lost to "Smooth," featuring Santana and Rob Thomas).

There was also a number of pay-per-view specials that continued to raise their profile and excite the throngs of fans who were unable to see an NSYNC concert but were tickled nonetheless to see the guys on screens at home, the biggest of which was the *'N Sync 'N Concert* special that debuted on pay-per-view in September 1999. The years that followed would present even more opportunities for the band, including lucrative deals with McDonald's, a Super Bowl halftime show, a *Saturday Night Live* showcase, and even the chance to be immortalized on *The Simpsons* and at Madame Tussauds Wax Museum.

But there was trouble brewing. For a band that was bringing in so much revenue and whose name was on the lips of fans and critics alike, they should have been bringing in bigger paychecks than what they had been receiving from Lou and Trans Continental Records. And when the band and their parents started looking into the discrepancies, everything suddenly took a very dark turn.

Gloria Estefan (center) joins NSYNC during VH1's Concert of the Century rehearsals in Washington, DC, in October 1999.

THE PROBLEM WITH PEARLMAN

"The sad thing is, Lou could have had it all. He could have had the new Motown in Orlando. But that's where greed comes in. He was just a really greedy person."

— Lance talking to *Billboard* in 2014

Maybe you've noticed in TV shows and movies that a dinner party always signals drama? Well, the same befell NSYNC when Lou invited Justin, JC, Joey, Chris, and Lance to gather for a band family meal—more specifically, a "check presentation dinner." And let's just say that the whole thing really left a bad taste in everyone's mouth.

It was late 1998, and NSYNC was raking in huge profits from the American release of their self-titled debut, the follow-up Christmas album, and their first, long-running headline tour. Lou wanted to celebrate, wrangling the guys and their parents for a lavish feast in Los Angeles, during which he'd give them their first big paycheck so they could all toast to the incredible success.

"We were all trying to guess what [the amount] would be, because we knew how much merch and how many records and how many tours we sold out," Lance recalled to *Billboard*. As each band member opened their envelope that night, they found a check written for a measly $10,000,

Chris, Joey, Lance, Justin, and JC pose in London in 1998.

which may seem like a lot of money but it was pennies compared to the millions NSYNC was bringing in. "I didn't want to seem ungrateful because at that point, yes, $10,000 was a lot of money," Lance told ABC's *20/20* in 2019, around the time *The Boy Band Con* was released, his documentary that delved deeper into the Pearlman debacle. "We went back to the hotel room and that's when it all just hit me. I was so disappointed. And I ripped up the check. . . . I knew something was wrong."

In fact, that $10,000 was less than a year's worth of the $35 per diem or "allowance" the guys had been receiving to that point. "Lou was making it seem like we were in so much debt that it would be a long time before we saw some real money," Lance said in *The Boy Band Con*, explaining how Lou gaslit and manipulated the guys into thinking their lack of funds was normal. "I was in the biggest band in the world and selling millions of records . . . but I can't even afford my apartment in Orlando. I couldn't even get a car," he added.

Lance's mom, Diane, also knew something was amiss. "My question was, 'How successful do you have to be before you start seeing, you know, some of the rewards for it?'" she said in VH1's *Driven*. Suddenly, the man the guys knew as "Papa Lou" was starting to become someone they didn't even know or recognize.

JC's uncle just so happened to be a lawyer and he started to take a deeper look at the contracts NSYNC and their parents signed early on in 1995. That same contract had been a deal breaker for short-lived member Jason Galasso who, in hindsight, was smart in refusing to sign it. Not only has Jason described it as a "phone-book thick"

document, but as he told the NSYNC podcast *The Digital Get Down,* he noticed a huge red flag within the pages too.

"[Lou] had himself written into the group not only for what he could recoup or what he could get, he also had himself written in there as if he was the sixth member of the group," Jason revealed. And therein lay the issue. Lou was able to take in 16.66 percent of the band's profits as a "sixth member," as well as padding in his fees for managing the group, which could be anywhere around 15–20 percent, according to *Billboard*, meaning Lou was making more than a third of the profits all on his own. It was, as JC's uncle has described it, "the worst contract I've ever read in my entire life."

Realizing how much they had been duped, NSYNC moved to find a way to fire Lou and get out of the atrocious contract that had tethered them to Lou and BMG for five full albums. There was a small loophole in the legalese that did, in fact, allow them to do so; according to *The Guardian*, there was "a buried clause in their contracts—that stipulated Pearlman had to sign the group to a US label (they were signed to a label within the German major BMG)—to declare it null and void." Discovering this huge flaw, NSYNC signed with Jive Records in July 1999. That was the new home of the Backstreet Boys, who had also recently discovered financial discrepancies with Lou in their similarly written contracts. BSB claimed they had only made $300,000 over the five years since the band's start in 1993, while they claimed Lou pocketed $10 million.

Like Backstreet Boys (and most other groups under the Pearlman talent umbrella), NSYNC also sued Lou and Trans Continental Records, claiming that the entity stole 50 percent of their rightful earnings. They issued a statement about their legal move, sharing, "Trans Continental's conduct with regard to 'N Sync is the most glaring, overt, and callous example of artist exploitation that the music industry has seen in a long time." In court documents, JC declared Lou "an unscrupulous, greedy, and sophisticated businessman who posed as an unselfish, loving father figure and took advantage of our trust."

Lou wasn't going to let his cash cow get away that easily. Trans Continental aligned with BMG and countersued, slapping NSYNC with a breach of contract lawsuit to the tune of $150 million, a document that also attempted to ban the boy band from recording any new music or performing under their now famous and well-known moniker. This ultimately meant delaying their forthcoming album, *No Strings Attached.*

"Basically, what we have here is a group that is signed to a multi-album contract. And this group has just walked across the street to a competing record company and signed a deal,"

Lou (back row, center) and Johnny (back row, fourth from the left) photographed with NSYNC and their families, circa 1996.

Lou and Trans Continental Records lawyer Michael Friedman told *New York Post* at the time. "'N Sync has shown very little regard for Lou Pearlman and their contract."

Lou also gave his own comments to the *Post*, sharing, "Personally, I'm sick over this. I've been in touch with the boys, and we're both not happy it had to resort to this legal battle. I care for them like a father cares for his sons."

MTV was in the Orlando courtroom when the trial began in 1999, noting that the members of NSYNC and Lou "dutifully ignored each other," as well as reporting on the throngs of fans that gathered outside the courthouse in a show of support. As the music channel reported, Judge Ann Conway denied the injunction, allowing NSYNC to continue working on new music.

The article added that "both parties met with a magistrate to discuss a possible settlement," which eventually did end up happening a short time later. But not before creating a lot of stress and trauma. "They were all really depressed. It had been so much fun up until that point and now reality set in," Lance's mom, Diane, told VH1. They still felt an allegiance to Lou but knew they had to break free if they were ever going to have a successful career and get paid fairly.

While the story of NSYNC, of course, went on to have a relatively happy ending, the same couldn't be said of Lou. Not long after the NSYNC battle played out very publicly, the FBI also looked into Mr. Pearlman and found that his nefarious activities were all part of an elaborate Ponzi scheme. As the US Securities and Exchange Commission explains it, a Ponzi scheme is "an investment fraud that pays existing investors with funds collected from new investors." Lou had been spinning a massive financial web of deceit for years,

including using boy bands as the bait to lure people to give him money—and it was finally catching up with him.

Lou was born in Flushing, New York, in 1954, to very humble beginnings. His father was a Jewish dry cleaner and his mother stayed at home raising the couple's only child. But there was another family member that enthralled young Lou and enticed him to want to get involved in the music business: his cousin, Art Garfunkel. As one half of the beloved folk group Simon & Garfunkel, Art enjoyed massive success throughout the '60s and '70s, and Lou wanted a piece of the same pie.

After graduating with a degree in accounting from Queens College in the late '70s, Lou quickly founded his first company and investment opportunity: a helicopter taxi fleet in his native New York. It led to a blimp-leasing operation, called Airship International (it didn't go off without a hitch, though, as the first blimp liftoff in 1980 crashed). Even so, Lou had been savvy—if not also scandalous—within the stock market realm, taking Airship International public and earning $3 million by 1985 in a "pump and dump scheme," says *Hollywood Reporter*.

For the first, but not only, time in his life, Lou would pick up his small fortune and run away, relocating from New York to Orlando by 1989, where he started convincing people to invest in his brand-new aviation business—Trans Continental. In fact, according to *Billboard*, "the jumbo jet pictured in the Trans Continental Airlines brochure was a toy airplane that once adorned his dresser." As the article goes on to explain, it was one of 84 businesses the scion established, also including pizza restaurants, steakhouses, and Chippendale's revues. In all of them, "investors contributed to the company's Employee Investment Savings

Accounts (EISA) program." Yet, "Every dollar went directly into [Lou's] deepening pockets."

At the same time, Lou was also leasing some of his planes to touring music acts, including NSYNC predecessors New Kids On The Block. When Lou realized the millions that boy band was bringing in, he harkened back to the extended family roots in music and pivoted to a new venture: Trans Continental Records. Building his musical roster started with an ad in the *Orlando Sentinel*, which netted him the Backstreet Boys. And once they got off the ground, he moved on, of course, to NSYNC, and then to the reality show *Making The Band*, which gave him O-Town. He also worked with LFO, Take 5, Aaron Carter, and even NKOTB's Jordan Knight, all of whom were signed to Lou's label at one point or another. Lou's billowing empire also included Trans Continental Studios, where he recorded many of the acts and his "Neverland-style ranch," reportedly a 16,000-square-foot mega mansion valued at $12 million, where he'd lure in both future boy banders and potential investors alike. Many of those investors were Florida retirees who handed over their life savings.

When the boy banders weren't after him, it was the government. In addition to lawsuits over lost profits, there were also a number of allegations of sexual assault from the talent pool that came to light in an explosive *Vanity Fair* exposé in 2007. By 2006, the FBI was onto Lou and had discovered the mogul had effectively run one of the longest and most

Federal agents raid Lou's offices at the Trans Continental Building in Orlando in February 2007.

Lou is brought to the George C. Young federal courthouse in Orlando on July 11, 2007.

one count of money laundering, and one count of making false statements. Lou was given a sentence of 300 months in prison (amounting to 25 years), symbolic of the $300 million he was convicted of pilfering. Eight years into his sentence, however, Lou died in prison, on August 19, 2016, of a heart attack.

Upon hearing the news, the members of NSYNC had mixed feelings. Of course, they were still upset with the man who took advantage of them and so many of their colleagues, but they were also reflective of how he had helped launch their careers. As Justin tweeted that day, "I hope he found some peace. God bless and RIP, Lou Pearlman." Chris also shared a statement on social media, posting, "Mixed emotions right now, but RIP Lou Pearlman." And Lance had some words as well: "Word is that #LouPearlman has passed away. He might not have been a standup businessman, but I wouldn't be doing what I love today w/out his influence. RIP Lou."

Before he passed away, Lou actually had every intention of finding another boy band act to get behind—trying to do the legwork behind prison bars. As *Billboard* noted, "Five days before his May 2008 sentencing, Pearlman issued a formal request to be permitted to develop bands while behind bars; all he would require was a telephone and an Internet connection two days a week." Of course, the judge and prosecutors presiding over his case scoffed at the idea and refused to allow such permissions.

"If I was given a chance to put another band together, that would have paid everybody back. But I never had that opportunity, and that's what was very upsetting," Lou told *Billboard* in 2014 in his first interview while in prison, eerily ending the chat with, "I'll be back."

ruthless Ponzi schemes in American history— a 20-year operation that bilked nearly 1,700 people collectively out of $300 million, with much of the money still missing.

By February 2007, the state of Florida raided Lou's house and took possession of his businesses, and Lou once again tried to run away from his problems, fleeing to a number of countries to try to evade capture. According to the *Orlando Sentinel*, he was spotted in Germany, Russia, Israel, Spain, Brazil, and Indonesia. By June 2007, he was apprehended in Bali and extradited back to the US, where he was convicted of two counts of conspiracy,

BEHIND THE BOY BAND CON

With America's collective interest in both boy bands and true crime, it was only a matter of time before a documentary was released detailing the salacious story of Lou Pearlman. It came in March 2019. Called *The Boy Band Con: The Lou Pearlman Story,* it first premiered at the prestigious SXSW Film Festival three years after Lou unceremoniously died in his prison cell. The hour-and-a-half tell-all (currently available for streaming on YouTube) was released under the umbrella of Lance Bass Productions, with the fifth and final member of NSYNC leading the charge to put out the movie. It was directed by Aaron Kunkel, who went on to complete other documentaries like the 2020 release *Bin Laden's Hard Drive.*

The exposé gathers a wealth of perspectives from those closest to Lou, including some of his childhood friends and associates, those who fell victim to his Ponzi scheme, and of course many of the boy band members at the center of it all. In addition to NSYNC's Lance, JC, and Chris, there's also Backstreet Boys' AJ McLean, O-Town's Ashley Parker Angel, Aaron Carter, and archive footage of the late Rich Cronin, who was part of LFO. Justin Timberlake's mom, Lynn, and Lance's mom, Diane, are also both featured in the film, and there are some recorded voiceover segments of Lou himself.

"When we started doing this, I didn't know half of the things that Lou was involved with, and all of the scams that he enacted. I was just floored by a lot of things that I learned," Lance told *Collider* around the time the documentary was released. "Ultimately, it's a cautionary tale that's so key to listen to, especially if you're going into the entertainment industry, as a young person or a family member of a young person. It gives you a nice warning of what to look out for, and you can use all of that information for really anything you're doing in life."

Throughout the film, a bevy of emotions come to the surface, consistent with how many felt about Lou—in particular, the boy banders themselves. "What we ended up with was just a very honest telling of his life. What I'm very excited about is that, at the end of the film, you feel as conflicted as all of us do, as far as how you're actually supposed to feel about Lou," Lance added in the *Collider* article. "As horrible as he was, as a businessman and scam artist, you still have this empathy for him, for some odd reason, and we wanted to tackle that."

Justin's mom, Lynn, also saw the more human side of Lou, sharing in the film, "I think deep down in his heart, that's what he really wanted to be—the sixth member of the group. I think he wanted those boys to see him that way too. And if he hadn't taken advantage of them, they would have."

NSYNC at the Arista Records
Pre-Grammy Awards party at
the Beverly Hills Hotel in February 2000.

GETTING SERIOUS WITH NO STRINGS ATTACHED

"None of us knew that was going to be the album of our lifetime."

— Lance chatting with *Entertainment Tonight* about *No Strings Attached* in 2020

After very publicly battling it out in an Orlando courtroom, in November 1999 NSYNC and Lou Pearlman decided to ultimately settle things quietly with mediators. By Christmas of that year, a statement was released announcing an amicable resolution.

Signed by the band, Trans Continental, BMG, and the Zomba Group (overseer of NSYNC's new label, Jive), it read, "All parties involved are extremely pleased with the speedy resolution of this matter. . . . 'N Sync will be able to build on the international success they have enjoyed with BMG and Trans Continental through a new worldwide recording contract with the Zomba Group's Jive Records."

In addition, NSYNC was able to keep their band name, and BMG was successful in inking a distribution deal with Jive that still allowed them a hefty piece of the NSYNC pie. There were also

A portrait of NSYNC from August 1999.

rumors that Lou was able to recoup on NSYNC's licensing and merchandising profits, although he did relinquish his "sixth band member" status as part of the deal.

Full details of the settlement have never been disclosed, as all parties signed a confidentiality agreement as part of the terms of the deal. But one thing was clear—"Papa Lou" was out as part of the NSYNC family. And Justin, JC, Joey, Chris, and Lance were ready to move on with a new era for the band. They did so with a big declaration of independence—the album *No Strings Attached.*

"*No Strings Attached* just became the theme," Chris told ABC's *20/20.* "It became our battle cry of, 'We don't owe anybody anymore . . . we have no ties to anything but each other . . . and our fans.'" In other interviews, Chris has shared that, initially, the idea for the album came from Disney, specifically the animated movie *Pinocchio* and the song, "I've Got No Strings," which plays the moment that the lovable lead character realizes his own freedom from Geppetto.

First announced in September 1999, *No Strings Attached* became a casualty of a number of legal delays, though that only added to the immense anticipation for NSYNC's follow-up to their 1998 debut. In January 2000, fans finally got the first single: the uber-hit "Bye Bye Bye." Even though it was intended by its songwriters as a more straightforward breakup song about a former flame, the song took on new meaning for NSYNC, deep into breaking things off with Lou.

"Bye Bye Bye" was officially released January 17, 2000, the very same night NSYNC performed it live at the *American Music Awards* and just a week after the official music video was released, all of which garnered a huge reaction. It was a moment of total triumph and maturity—and it signaled a band to be taken seriously in the music milieu of the new millennium. "Boy bands were still an easy punchline for much of the population . . . but it was clear even grown-ups were starting to pay attention to *NSYNC," *Stereogum* has said of the "Bye Bye Bye" era, adding, "It was clear 2000 would be *NSYNC's year."

Sure enough, "Bye Bye Bye" became an overnight success. It had an immediate grip on radio, retail, and cultural curators like MTV's *TRL* (where it stayed in top rotation for 65 days). It peaked at No. 4 on the *Billboard Hot 100* chart and stayed within the top rankings for 23 weeks. *Rolling Stone* included the song at number six on its list of the 50 Greatest Boy Band Songs of All Time, saying, "It remains their defining track, a four-minute blast of big hooks, tight harmonies, and intriguingly meta subtext."

What is even more remarkable is that the song almost didn't happen at all.

"Bye Bye Bye" was written by NSYNC's longtime Swedish collaboration team, led by Max Martin (Denniz Pop had sadly passed away by this point). With the help of an ensemble of hitmakers (and fellow Swedes) Andreas Carlsson, Rami Yacoub, and Kristian Lundin, Max and company once again helped architect the two biggest hits on the boy band's new album. In addition to "Bye Bye

Hitclips, which played short snippets of popular songs, for some of the biggest artists of the early 2000s, including for NSYNC's "Bye Bye Bye."

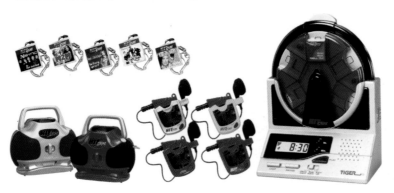

Bye" (originally offered to British boy band 5ive, who passed on it), they also came up with the blockbuster track, "It's Gonna Be Me."

But it was a nail-biting back-and-forth battle getting Max to commit to NSYNC. The notable music man had a big reputation to uphold and was concerned about the implications of NSYNC's trial with Lou and BMG. The last thing he wanted was to be entangled in the legal tryst.

It was an incredibly tenuous time all around. As JC remembered in *Billboard*, "We literally thought our [career was] ending . . . [we were] under an incredible amount of pressure to get ['Bye Bye Bye'] out, because we were afraid we were going to be forgotten. . . . we were genuinely worried."

Manager Johnny Wright stepped in and worked his magic (and a bit of manipulation), pulling on the heartstrings of Max to convince him to give NSYNC the rights to "Bye Bye Bye" (which the boy band had first recorded with the Swedes in early 1999). Specifically, Johnny put big collateral on the table, telling Max that NSYNC had an opportunity to play the Radio Music Awards in late October 1999 and needed a big hit to ensure the future of their career. "I pleaded with Max and his team, like, 'Look, this could be the final time that the fans see the group,'" Johnny recalled to *Billboard* in an oral history of *No Strings Attached*.

"I knew if we performed it, it would be etched in the fans' minds as our song," Johnny added. And he was right. With Max's blessing, NSYNC got the track and debuted it for the first time at that pivotal Radio Music Awards gig, just weeks shy of the court fracas kicking off in Orlando. "Over the course of this court battle, people were replaying the performance. Fan base strength started growing, and this was

Producer Kevin Briggs at the 2000 Grammy Awards. Briggs contributed the song "It Makes Me Ill" to NSYNC's *No Strings Attached.*

kind of like the flagship song as everybody was getting news on the court battle from MTV," Johnny recalled.

MTV also played the infamous music video for "Bye Bye Bye" ad nauseum (as of publication, it's just shy of 350 million views on YouTube), and like the song, the visual accompaniment made a statement. In it, each of the five guys appears as puppets on strings in a marionette show, controlled by a larger-than-life figure that looms above. The stage is also decorated with the phrase "*libertas,*" Latin for *freedom.* Eventually, the strings are cut and the guys are able to run, drive, and maneuver away from their manipulator, though she doesn't give up without a fight. The whole thing comes off like a mini-Hollywood blockbuster movie, made on a cool $1 million budget.

One of the most iconic parts of the video is that it introduced the band's signature dance move (the talk-back gesture across the chest followed by the fist in the air power punch) that has now become synonymous with NSYNC's image and cultural legacy. To develop the dance, they turned to boy band go-to choreographer Darrin Henson. Henson recalled to *Entertainment Weekly* that the sequence combined an iteration on the iconic black power fist with a maneuver that symbolized silencing the oppressor. "I come from the Bronx, and in New York whenever somebody said something, you'd put your hand up in a talking manner, like open and close, meaning, 'stop talking shit,'" he shared.

The hype that "Bye Bye Bye" garnered and the newsworthiness of the public legal battle on its heels set up *No Strings Attached* to be a very fortuitous album, allowing the band to get the last laugh in the war against their former Svengali. "It was the marketing/press campaign money couldn't buy," Jive Records' Barry Weiss told *Entertainment Tonight*. "It created an inordinate amount of pent-up demand in the marketplace, so when the album came out, it was a volcanic explosion of sales."

In fact, when *No Strings Attached* was finally released on March 21, 2000, it sold 2.41 million copies in its first week, including 1.1 million on release day alone. It set a new record for first-week sales (one that would not be broken for 15 years), and the album stayed in the No. 1 spot on the *Billboard* charts for eight consecutive weeks (and 82 weeks total across the *Billboard 200*). It would go on to be certified 11x Platinum by the Recording Industry Association of America®. It remains the band's biggest-selling record.

RIGHT: NSYNC fans at the Rose Bowl in Pasadena, California, watch the band perform in June 2000.

INSET: A 2001 Best Buy ad for popular CDs, including a great deal on *No Strings Attached*.

Not only did *No Strings Attached* set "an industry standard," per *Billboard*, but it beat out NSYNC's stiffest competition, the Backstreet Boys, breaking that band's 1999 record for sales of *Millennium,* which netted 1.134 million copies in its first week. *No Strings Attached* also blew well past benchmarks made by other big albums of 2000, including Britney Spears' *Oops! . . . I Did It Again* and Eminem's *The Marshall Mathers LP*, which sold a respective 1.3 and 1.7 million units in their debut weeks.

Part of the bonanza was the huge effect of the NSYNC army, as Jive Records senior VP of sales and marketing Tom Carrabba recalled to *Billboard*: "We had fan lists—we accumulated hundreds of thousands of names and addresses. We were documenting everything and utilizing it. So every time we went back to the market, we had an army of people we could contact." Not to mention there were huge marketing and advertising campaigns at the time, including deals with Verizon Wireless and Chili's (remember that ubiquitous "Baby Back Ribs" commercial with the guys on the deserted island?). All of it kept NSYNC front and center of many minds.

The year 2000 was, overall, a curious time. Not only was it a huge turning point for humankind, as people the world over celebrated the fact that they had "survived" the doomsday narrative of Y2K, but also a huge changing of the guard for music too. Pop reigned supreme, with Christina, Britney, and other *Mickey Mouse Club* veterans hitting it big, while the Backstreet Boys still had a stronghold and Destiny's Child were coming around the bend.

And people (in particular young people) were buying music like it was a necessity. On the release day of *No Strings Attached,* for example, NSYNC fans lined up for blocks at their local record stores (and some locations remained open until midnight just to handle the overflow). The Virgin Megastore in New York City had an unexpected 8,000 fans show up (several hundred of whom camped out on the sidewalks overnight) for the band's in-store appearance on release day, after many learned about the event in AOL chatrooms.

"It was just *NSYNC mania that day," Janet Kleinbaum, Jive's VP of artist marketing, told *Billboard* of the mammoth success of the album's release day sales. "Every city, every town, every fan went to their local place to get that album. I was getting calls and notes from . . . all my colleagues at all different record labels. It was incredible. Nobody has seen anything like that before." Kleinbaum adds that many people bought multiple copies, even in a time long before today's well-marketed collector variants at retail outlets.

According to the Recording Industry Association of America®, the fact that *No Strings Attached* rolled out in 2000 was very much a "right place, right time" phenomenon. It was a pinnacle year for CD sales in the country, with $13.2 billion in music sales driven by the format alone (accounting for 92.3 percent of sales). Every year since

Houston fans cheer as NSYNC performs at a tour stop in May 2000.

2000, the percentage of CD sales has largely decreased due to digital advancements.

In fact, had *No Strings Attached* been released just one year later, the advent of Napster and other music file-sharing sites might have wholly prevented the album's acceleration. In 2001, Napster hit its high point, as 1.5 million people were sharing music (for free!) using the technology. While the platform didn't wholly end up affecting NSYNC's 2001 follow-up, *Celebrity,* which sold about 1.8 million in its first week, there's no denying it helped create discord for many artists around 2001–2004, NSYNC included. It makes it all

the more apropos that Justin gunned to play Napster founder Sean Parker in the 2010 movie *The Social Network*. As one person opined on Reddit, "Justin Timberlake was so disgruntled by N Sync's songs being pirated on Napster, he took up acting with the goal of portraying Sean Parker as a 'huge douchebag.'"

What was also compelling about *No Strings Attached* was that, stylistically, it was a diversion from NSYNC's earlier self-titled debut, incorporating elements of R&B, new jack swing, and hip-hop in addition to pop, and veering away from the formulaic bubblegum undertones of its predecessor.

NSYNC in their iconic *No Strings Attached* looks at the MTV Movie Awards in 2000.

LEFT: Richard Marx in 1989.

RIGHT: Diane Warren in 1999.

After "Bye Bye Bye" came the funky pop number "It's Gonna Be Me" as the second single, released May 16, 2000; it was in the No. 1 spot on the *Billboard Hot 100* chart for two weeks and spent 25 weeks total rotating spots. And its blowhorn chorus and over-pronunciation live on as a meme, celebrating the changing of the month at the end of April. The video—depicting the NSYNCers as larger-than-life dolls—is also one of their better efforts. Like "Bye Bye Bye," it was directed by Wayne Isham.

The third and final single from *No Strings Attached* was "This I Promise You," a heart-melting ballad that debuted September 19, 2000, peaked at No. 5 on the *Billboard Hot 100*, and spent over 26 weeks on the chart. It was such a hit, a Spanish-language version—"Yo te Voy a Amar"—was distributed to international

markets and the guys performed it live at the Latin Grammys in 2001.

Elsewhere on the album, there were futuristic electronic romps and an early use of Autotune in the very *not* PG "Digital Get Down" (in which JC foreshadows online dating), heavy drum lines in "Bringin' Da Noise," and rapping and beatboxing in parts. This was not the late '90s NSYNC anymore. "There's a little more edge to this album, a little more grit," Justin, who also famously raps over the breakdown of "Just Got Paid," told *Rolling Stone*. "We're pissed off now—that's what it is. We're angry white boys who didn't get our props," he added, before pulling back, "No, I'm kidding."

But was he?

As the people in the recording studio have attested to, there was a huge drive in the five guys of NSYNC as they put together the material for *No Strings Attached*. "There was definitely a cloud that went away—and it was a cloud that nobody knew was there until it was gone and the sun came out," one of the composers/producers Alex Greggs told *Entertainment Tonight*. He added that much of the album was recorded in a modest house in Florida (a sliver of the excess of Lou's theme park compound) that JC and Joey moved into during sessions. Said Alex, "Once we were in the studio, there was a whole new energy. There was some fight in them."

There was also new personnel working with NSYNC this time around. Beyond those important Swedish stalwarts, *No Strings Attached* also features some curious new blood, including well-known '80s pop rock star Richard Marx, who wrote "This I Promise You." (Curiously, JC once nailed a childhood talent contest singing Richard's "Right Here Waiting"). Songwriter extraordinaire Diane Warren scribed the track "That's When I'll Stop Loving You." There was also TLC/Destiny's Child mastermind Kevin "She'kspere" Briggs, who contributed the song "It Makes Me Ill."

But perhaps the writing talent that shone the brightest on the album was JC himself. JC has writing credits for the first track, "Space Cowboy (Yippie-Yi-Yay)" (along with TLC's Lisa "Left Eye" Lopes), as well as "Digital Get Down" and "Bringin' Da Noise" (both alongside NSYNC's early co-writer Veit Renn). Justin and Chris also received credits for "Just Got Paid," their reworking of the 1988 hit by Johnny Kemp that they assembled alongside Teddy Riley and Aaron Hall. The line-up shows the bootstrap way the album was created, especially when things were tenuous with Lou and BMG, and NSYNC didn't even know if they would have a label behind the record.

"The record company didn't send anyone to us. It was a sticky situation," JC told *Rolling Stone*. "A lot of creative people we approached didn't want to work with us. We didn't have a contract saying that any of these songs would make it on the album when we did get a new deal. So the people who worked with us were straight up about the music. And that was amazing." He added, "This is our record. We hired the people we wanted to hire."

Critics were quick to notice the difference, with a unanimous chorus of praise for an album that was the opposite of a sophomore slump. *AllMusic* called it a "vast improvement on the debut," adding that "Bye Bye Bye" is "a piledriving dance number with the catchiest chorus they've ever sang." Furthermore, said the review, "*No Strings Attached* pulls away from the standard dance-pop formula, strengthening it with harder street beats, electronica flourishes, ballads with some grit, and well-crafted pop tunes."

The *New York Times* added that *No Strings Attached* was "flush with artistic freedom" and compared the style to the Rolling Stones coming across 1950s blues. Like great 1980s R&B, the review asserted, "[It] balances pretty melody atop hip-hop's street level beat."

Consequence of Sound said the album "proves the power of exploring new genres," adding, "there is something about the work as a whole that moves away from standard pop, leaning into, instead, a musical genre that had dominated the previous millennium: hip-hop. . . . In a way, the band changed their ways, slightly loosening their grip on the popdom that initially landed them on the musical map and instead embracing something slightly different. By doing so, 'N Sync was catapulted to new heights of fame."

WHAT WAS THE ALBUM THAT PULLED STRINGS FROM THE TOP?

Eventually, all good things come to an end, and the blockbuster first-week sales record that NSYNC enjoyed with *No Strings Attached* was toppled in 2015. The culprit? Adele. The British songbird's third album, *25*, which featured the huge hit single "Hello," was released on November 20, 2015, and sold 2.43 million copies in just four days. It bested NSYNC's record for 2.41 million copies sold in a debut week. Not that there were any hard feelings.

As Joey told *Billboard,* "Adele is the truth . . . kinda excited a rare talent like hers is in the same breath as our group," adding, "Records are always meant to be broken." Lance shared on social media, "Congratulations," following it up with the joke hashtag #IDemandARecount. And JC posted on X, formerly known as Twitter, "Well done Adele."

Although Justin didn't publicly comment on the record-breaking moment, manager Johnny Wright recalled the singer's reaction to *Billboard*: "Justin was like, 'Yo, she's the shit. She deserves it.' It was refreshing to know that there was still a fan base out there that would buy great music."

Of course, post-*No Strings Attached*, there were plenty of other albums with big returns in their first week, too, including Taylor Swift records *1989* (1.28 million copies), *Red* (1.20 million copies), and *Speak Now* (1.04 million copies); Lady Gaga's *Born This Way* (1.10 million copies); and even Backstreet Boys' *Black & Blue* (1.59 million copies).

But the 2-million mark is an unparalleled feat that few besides NSYNC (and Adele) have ever been able to achieve. As Johnny said, "No one will ever be able to replace the energy and how the whole thing went down with [*No Strings Attached*]."

NSYNC performs on the No Strings Attached Tour in 2000.

Stereogum has also heaped praise on *No Strings Attached* in retrospective reviews, noting, "It's hard to think of an album that does the boy-band formula better," and saying, "it deserved to be massive on the strength of pop songcraft and performance. . . . Twenty years later, the thing just sparkles."

No Strings Attached would go on to be nominated for several Grammy Awards, including Best Pop Vocal Album, Record of the Year, and Best Pop Performance by a Duo or Group with Vocal for "Bye Bye Bye." (Unfortunately, NSYNC lost to U2 for Record of the Year and Steely Dan for the other two categories.)

Jive Records put all their marketing muscle behind the album, scheduling NSYNC for a number of high-profile appearances. Ahead of the album release day, the boy band appeared on *Saturday Night Live* on March 11, 2000, in an episode hosted by *Dawson's Creek* actor Joshua Jackson. "If you're a teenage girl, I'm fairly confident you've heard of me and also the music guest NSYNC," Jackson said in his monologue, his assertion met with uproarious applause.

During their performance segments, NSYNC offered "Bye Bye Bye" and the more demure five-part-harmony track "I Thought She Knew," written by their longtime vocal coach Robin Wiley. It was NSYNC's one and only *SNL* appearance, though Justin of course would go on to host and/or appear numerous times over the following two decades, including the most

GETTING SERIOUS WITH *NO STRINGS ATTACHED* 105

In Sync with NSYNC

Trying to put into words what NSYNC means to me is no easy task. In the summer of 1998, my television landed on the Disney Channel. I heard "Hi, we're NSYNC," and from that very moment, my life changed. Just like many teenage girls vowed their eternal love and support for the band, I swore I'd love them forever. That night and to this day, the harmonies, the music, and, most importantly, the brotherhood set them apart from the other boy bands of the era. Nearly three decades, eight NSYNC concerts, and hundreds of related events later, the experiences I've had are some of the core memories of my life. From my first show in 1999 when I cried just breathing the same air as my five favorites, to seeing their last public performance of the national anthem at their 2004 Challenge for the Children basketball game, to booking a six-hour cross-country flight to see them reunite in 2018 to get their star, the five members of NSYNC hold a cherished place in my heart. Nothing made me more proud than hearing "Better Place" in 2023. I look forward to what the thirtieth anniversary of the band will bring us!

Christine Yando

recent stint in January 2024 to promote his new song, "Selfish."

Soon after the March 2000 appearance on *SNL*, NSYNC also headed to the 72nd annual Academy Awards telecast, performing the Best Original Song nominee "Music of My Heart" with collaborator Gloria Estefan. The band also had countless appearances on MTV, ABC's daytime talk show *The View* and *The Tonight Show with Jay Leno*, and a prime spot on *Good Morning America*, in which the fan screams were so loud it was hard to even make out what the guys were saying during

their interview. NSYNC also graced the cover of the March 2000 issue of *Rolling Stone*.

As James Grandoni, VP of purchasing at National Record Mart, told *Entertainment Weekly* of the massive PR blitz behind *No Strings Attached*, "You had to be deaf, dumb, and blind not to know that this record was coming out."

And then there was the tour. Like the album, the No Strings Attached Tour broke incredible records, selling 1 million tickets in its first day (it was announced the same day the album came out on March 21, 2000). The 50-plus-date tour was completely sold out; it began May 9, 2000, in Biloxi, Mississippi, and wrapped up December 1, 2000, in San Diego.

Most shows were held at large stadiums and arenas that were flooded with fans. Openers included a range of one-hit wonders, but also future chart-topper Pink on a number of dates. According to MTV, NSYNC sold the most tickets of any tour in 2000, though, in terms of total gross, they came just behind Tina Turner for the top spot. The No Strings Attached Tour netted $76.4 million when all was said and done.

Critical reviews of the tour were favorable. In a recap of a show in NSYNC's hometown, the *Orlando Sentinel* wrote, "The power of this concert was in its impeccable production. It was an assault on the senses from the moment the five singers were lowered to the stage as human marionettes for the opening 'No Strings Attached.'" The writer also praised the tour's "pyrotechnics, lasers, moving sidewalks, elaborate videos, and a detachable mini-stage that took the band into the midst of the audience."

And although *New York Daily News* softly panned some of the "worn clichés of current teen pop," the writer did herald the boy band's "personal charm [and] musical appeal," adding, "Onstage, the guys exude a niceness that's engaging. Their five-part harmonies really sparkle in the ballads . . . And their ace a cappella work on 'I Thought She Knew' puts them in the tradition of pop's most pleasing harmonizers, from the barbershop quartets through the doo-woppers."

The New York run of shows—held at the world-famous Madison Square Garden—were filmed for an HBO pay-per-view special; it brought in 6 million viewers (a first for the network) and was nominated for a *TV Guide* Award for Music Special of the Year, further setting up NSYNC for the fast-growing *Celebrity* that was about to come.

Yet, like most things for NSYNC, the tour was not without its fair share of drama. At one date, a female fan climbed 70 feet of stage rigging in an attempt to be up close and personal with the guys. "She jumped to the rigging ladder, shimmied down, got to the top of the stage, went down (another) ladder, and got right next to us. We were just staring at her. It was funny at the time, but, wow, she could have gotten hurt," Lance told *Entertainment Weekly*.

In Illinois, Mother Nature had it in for NSYNC, as a tornado tore through the speedway in which the boy band was supposed to play and ultimately destroyed the stage. The date was rescheduled but even that had a hiccup; parents who sat in traffic for upward of four hours with crying kids who missed the show attempted to sue the speedway and promoters for the mess on the second go-around.

One of the most serious developments could have happened at the Atlanta show: a 17-year-old apparently had plans to assassinate the members of NSYNC. A notebook detailed his manifesto, which included plans to rob a gun shop in his home state of Tennessee and travel to the arena to carry out his plan. Thankfully, the boy's mother found the writings and turned in her son to authorities. Per *Rolling Stone*'s reporting on the event, "As for a motive, apparently as the concert approached the teenager became frustrated hearing his female classmates discuss the band, the concert, and which members they liked best."

BECOMING A BIG CELEBRITY

"People have labeled us as not bein' artistic, but after this album I don't think we'll hear 'boy band' too much more. We're trying to grow musically. We're trying to take that step where no boy band has gone before."

—Justin talking to *Rolling Stone* about *Celebrity* in 2001

At the end of 2000, NSYNC were cultural demigods deemed wholly responsible for "shaking up the sound of Y2K pop" (*Billboard*), and they wanted to strike again while the iron was hot. So, with the red-hot flames of *No Strings Attached* barely extinguished, the five members of the boy band eyed the record's follow-up.

"It actually feels like we've been away for a little while. We average an album a year, basically, and it's been working for us so far, so why not?" Lance told *Entertainment Weekly* about the rush to put out another album. Plus, he said, "Right now, in this time, if you disappear for too long, you kind of get forgotten."

In December 2000, after wrapping up the massive $76 million No Strings Attached Tour, NSYNC appeared on the red carpet of the *Billboard* Music Awards, spilling the tea about some new

The guys, circa 2001.

NSYNC performs live at the 2000 *Billboard* Music Awards.

material. "We're going to spend January and February [2001] in [the studio] and see what we can come up with," Justin told MTV ahead of the award show telecast. Once again, it was time to cue the band headlines, tempting fans to stay glued to chatrooms, teen mags, and *TRL* for breaking news.

Behind the scenes, NSYNC were taking a more serious approach to determining how to move forward with what would become their fourth and (to-date) final album, *Celebrity*. Whereas *No Strings Attached* had a mission—to gain back control from their overlord—*Celebrity* eyed precisely how NSYNC would define themselves as they stepped further out of the shadows. More than any other album, it was their chest-pumping R-E-S-P-E-C-T moment.

"Our objective was not to be self-conscious and try to make another hit record. Instead, we set out to make a record that was more

reflective of what turns us on musically. We also wanted to prove that pop music comes in a lot of different flavors. It's not all bubble-gum," JC told *Billboard* at the time.

There was also a feeling of having to prove themselves to critics. Although *No Strings Attached* brought in huge acclaim and positive reviews, there were still the naysayers and a league of music snobbery that dismissed the group as nothing more than a flash-in-the-pan boy band manufactured to appeal to the whims of hormone-fueled teenagers and preteens.

As Justin said in the same interview with JC, "The truth is that it can be tiresome to be continually blasted by critics because we don't fit their preconceived notion of what a 'credible' group is. I wonder if they listen to our music before venturing an opinion."

To assert themselves even further as a bona fide music act, NSYNC brought in the big guns for *Celebrity*. Other than two songs ("Just Don't Tell Me That" and "Tell Me, Tell Me . . . Baby"), gone were the Swedish godfathers who had blessed NSYNC with huge hits. In their places were Pharrell Williams and Chad Hugo of the songwriting and production duo the Neptunes, who helped craft the single "Girlfriend," crooner Brian McKnight, and the band's choreographer/dancer-turned songwriter Wade Robson, who had initially penned *Celebrity*'s title track for his own album but gifted it to NSYNC. Wade also added to "Pop," "Gone," and "See Right Through You." Heck, even Stevie Wonder appears in a harmonica cameo on the song "Something Like You."

But the writing duo that garnered much of the credit for *Celebrity* was none other than Justin and JC. With *Celebrity,* the two realized their dream of becoming a songwriting team,

an idea first hatched after the cancellation of *The All-New Mickey Mouse Club* six years earlier. Across *Celebrity*'s thirteen tracks, Justin has seven writing credits (the most of any contributor on the album) while JC has four, further emblematic of how "the group's sound and leadership had shifted decisively" by the time the album was being made, says *Billboard*. And perhaps it was also this taste of power that led to NSYNC's downfall. Could the allure of the studio magic have been the deciding factor that pushed Justin into pursuing his own endeavors as a solo artist?

NSYNC also did a curious thing with the music on *Celebrity*—they previewed half of it on tour before the record even came out. In May 2001, the band embarked on the dazzling spectacle known as the PopOdyssey Tour, performing six tracks from the then-

The Neptunes (Chad Hugo, left, and Pharrell Williams, right) in 2003.

unreleased record each night to tens of thousands of fans. Like "Bye Bye Bye," the titillating tease once again paid off, leading to breathless anticipation for the forthcoming record. As Jive's Barry Weiss told *Billboard*, "The fact that audiences are responding so well so immediately to these new songs in this setting is incredible. It indicates to us that we've got an album of immeasurable creative and commercial depth."

The first *Celebrity* single officially came on May 14, 2001: the digital dance breakdown "Pop" (it peaked on the *Billboard Hot 100* at No. 19 and spent 15 weeks on the chart). It was a commentary on pop music in general, meant to take on an air of a rock anthem for their own genre, as JC explained to *Entertainment Weekly*: "You know how Joan Jett had 'I Love Rock & Roll,' or Twisted Sister and Kiss had their anthems? It's always about rock & roll. And pop's never really had an anthem." A music video also was released, again directed by Wayne Isham; curiously, Joey does not appear in it, as he injured himself at a concert rehearsal the night prior to the video shoot. (He's replaced by Wade Robson.)

"Pop" features the electronic wizardry of DJ and producer BT (real name Brian Transeau), who JC basically staked out at a number of the "dirty pop" beatmaker's shows to invite him to collaborate. BT's studio flourishes are heard throughout the four-minute headturner, with more than 30 seconds of it devoted solely to Justin's beatboxing. It's a style choice that has been a source of much soapboxing over the years, and just more fodder for those who have criticized the superstar for often appropriating Black culture (his once hairstyle choice of cornrows certainly didn't help). *Rolling Stone* even describes Justin in this context with a

Celebrity-era feature, calling him "the Southern boy with a bunch of black in him . . . [he] is with the black bodyguards, wearing a Jimi Hendrix T-shirt, watching Spike Lee's concert film *The Original Kings of Comedy* on a portable DVD player."

But in fact, Justin never wanted the beatboxing to appear anywhere on the record. The story goes that BT caught Justin in the act while doing vocal warmups for a studio session and pleaded with him to record it. "I'm like, 'Dude, that's dope. You gotta go in there and do that!'" the producer told *Rolling Stone*. "[Justin's] like, 'No, I never put that on our tracks.' I'm like, 'I don't give a shit, dude! Get your ass in there.'" The band liked it so much they kept the beatboxing in the demo given to Jive. But the label hated it, and at first was reluctant to bank on "Pop" as the anchor to get behind as the first single for *Celebrity*.

"They were like, 'I don't know. I don't like that song. I don't think you should go there. It's too different,'" Lance said, per *Reuters*. But the band stuck to their guns with the execs: "And we're like, 'No, that's what we want to do. We don't want to do 10 'Bye Bye Byes' or three 'God Must Have Spents,'" Lance continued. "That's why every song on this album is different from each other. And they're all . . . cool."

It was a wise decision. At the time, the boy band craze was beginning to crash. Per *Entertainment Weekly*, it was the start of the "Teen Bust," when album sales of the genre were taking a nosedive and, according to *Reuters,* even "disappointing box-office returns and ratings for youth-targeted movies and TV shows [were] evidence of a downward spiral."

NSYNC were highly intuitive and knew they had to do something different to break out from

NSYNC and host Kathy Griffin (center) present an award at the 2000 *Billboard* Music Awards.

the pack and stay afloat. *Celebrity* was their playground to sandbox different music styles. In fact, the release of *Celebrity*, originally slated for June 2001, ended up being delayed by a month, to allow the guys and their producers du jour more time to perfect the album.

The move paid off. When it was released on July 24, 2001, *Celebrity* was another bullseye in the NSYNC canon. Though it didn't net the record-breaking first-week sales of *No Strings Attached*, it still hit an impressive 1.87 million units sold, which was regarded at the time as the second-best debut week for any American album. "Honestly, if we sell 2 million records in the first week, and some newspaper comes out and says we're falling off, I'm gonna laugh the shit out of myself," Justin joked early on with *Entertainment Weekly*.

In fact, *Celebrity* was the best-selling pop album of 2001, with a total of 4.42 million copies sold, and the overall No. 3 album of the year; metal-rap hybrid act Linkin Park and reggae star

Shaggy took the No. 1 and 2 spots, respectively. *Celebrity* would go on to be certified 5x Platinum by the Recording Industry Association of America® for 5 million units sold.

Celebrity also ruled the *Billboard* charts, spending one week at No. 1 and 43 total weeks on the *Billboard 200*. And, like *No Strings Attached*, the artwork (featuring a photo by *Rolling Stone*'s premier photographer Mark Seliger) made an overt statement. No longer puppets on strings, the five guys were strutting their newfound fame on a red carpet with paparazzi and screaming fans lined up alongside them. "Everybody knows we like to make fun of ourselves, so we're taking a stab at the word 'celebrity,'" Lance told *Entertainment Weekly* about the concept. "The cover is very glammed out and 'ooh, superstar.' And then on the inside it shows what the real 'glamorous' life is in this business—sleeping in airports and all of that."

Yet they really tapped into the album's overarching theme, at least with a star-

The band and their wax lookalikes at
Madame Tussauds New York in 2002.

studded album release party that July at Hollywood hot spot Club Moomba. Among the guests were Hugh Hefner, the Olsen twins, and, of course, Britney Spears.

Two more singles (and popular music videos) would soon be delivered in the form of the sultry serenade "Gone" on August 21, 2001 (peaking on the *Billboard Hot 100* at No. 11, with 24 weeks logged on the chart), and the R&B bedroom stunner "Girlfriend" on January 14, 2002 (peaking at No. 5 on the charts with 20 weeks total in the rankings). Curiously, both songs also moved NSYNC into new chart territory by placing on *Billboard*'s Hot R&B/Hip-Hop Songs list. "Gone" peaked at No. 14 and spent 20 weeks total in the rankings; "Girlfriend" peaked at No. 23 and also spent 20 weeks on the chart.

"Gone" is also notable for being the first NSYNC song where Justin is in total command, taking all the lead vocals and once again giving him a taste of the solo limelight. "I think it's the first idea I ever got about doing something on my own, because it was the first time I have ever really felt the confidence to do it," Justin once said in an interview with Oprah. *Billboard* even asserted the song "established Timberlake as a solo artist long before he was actually a solo artist, and remains one of his very best singles to date."

NSYNC performs with Michael Jackson and former members of the Jackson 5 at Jackson's 30th anniversary concert in 2001.

But "Gone" was also of the finer moments for NSYNC in total, showing their raw potential. As JC told *Billboard*, "[It's] about as raw as it gets. It's just us and a beatbox, with just a tiny accent of acoustic guitar and violin. That song is a proud moment for us; it really shows how tight we are as a group."

The song was originally penned by Justin (with Britney in mind) and co-writer Wade Robson, and it was intended for Michael Jackson. He passed on it, but later changed his mind, wanting to do a duet with Justin, but the request came too late, as the track had already been released. Yet the King of Pop's influence was clearly evident all over *Celebrity*

at a time when the two music acts were really crossing paths.

MJ has long been an influence on Justin; as he once said, "To create the things that [Michael] created with his music is untouchable. He opened the minds of the world to be able

ABOVE: NSYNC performs with Aerosmith and Britney Spears during the halftime show for Super Bowl XXXV on January 28, 2001.

INSET: The "Girlfriend" single.

to do that through his music . . . [it's] a feat not accomplished by many people, maybe only a handful of people. I don't think anyone ever did it like him."

On the flipside, Michael was pushing Justin to work with him, perhaps in a way to elevate Michael's own career in the new millennium by teaming with a giant in a younger generation. Either way, it was the beginning of a sweet bond between the King and the pop princes. At the 2001 MTV Music Video Awards, Jackson made a surprise appearance after NSYNC's performance and the boy band also helped induct the legend into the Rock & Roll Hall of Fame that same year.

Overall, critics were largely in favor of NSYNC's stylistic moves on *Celebrity*, even while many still panned boy band-driven pop music in general. *Slant* went so far as to say "NSYNC could make the brave step toward becoming the Beatles of their generation" if they kept experimenting and growing with their aging-out fan base. And *Rolling Stone* exclaimed, "'N Sync are paving a new high road for teen pop's future" while saying *Celebrity* "goes several steps further outside the proven boy-band sphere."

NSYNC was also nominated again for Grammys for their work on *Celebrity*, with the album included for consideration as Best Pop Vocal Album and "Gone" nominated for Best Pop Performance by a Duo or Group with Vocals at the 44th annual award show. NSYNC once again lost to U2 for the latter and Sade for the former. Because "Girlfriend" was released as a single in January 2002, it was up for consideration at the 45th annual Grammy Awards that year, nominated for Best Pop Performance by a Duo or Group with Vocal; the band performed it live with

special guest Nelly during the telecast (the rapper also appeared on an official remix). NSYNC lost in that category to No Doubt. To date, they have never won a Grammy, though they have been nominated eight times total.

But it did nothing to detract from the band's hugely successful year in 2001. In addition to the global success of *Celebrity* that year, bringing about appearances on *The Rosie O'Donnell Show* and *The Today Show,* among others, NSYNC was immortalized in Barbie dolls and at Madame Tussauds Wax Museum; appeared at the Super Bowl XXXV Halftime Show alongside Aerosmith in a featurette dubbed "The Kings of Rock and Pop," along with spots from Nelly, Mary J. Blige, and Justin's girlfriend, Britney Spears (whose relationship was so top level at this point it resulted in death threats); had endorsement deals with McDonald's; appeared on an episode of *The Simpsons*; had individual covers on the August 2021 edition of *Rolling Stone;* and had one of the biggest tours of the year.

The PopOdyssey Tour kicked off May 23, 2001, and ran through September 1, 2001, playing huge stadiums like Soldier Field in Chicago and Giants Stadium in New Jersey, just outside New York City. It was considered the "biggest production in pop music" at the time, with a massive stage setup (so much so the tour had to be pushed back a week to add more time to build it), plus pyro, fireworks, suspension, and video graphics. The overhead was covered by big sponsors Verizon and Chili's. It was also the first time NSYNC was joined by backup dancers. Openers included a range of pop acts like Debbie Gibson, Christina Milian, and Eden's Crush.

Justin with his marionette at FAO Schwarz in New York City in 2000.

As the *Toronto Sun* described it in a review, the epic show featured a "five-storey-high stage with three video screens, state-of-the-art circular speakers and lights straight out of *Close Encounters of the Third Kind*," yet the concept was based on another famous movie, as Lance told *Entertainment Weekly*: "It was a play on *2001: A Space Odyssey*. We wanted to pay tribute to pop icons. So the whole tour revolves around the meaning of pop and what was popular from the '40s till today."

It was the second-biggest tour of 2001, just behind U2 and just in front of the Backstreet Boys. In total, the PopOdyssey Tour brought in $90 million. Industry magazine *Pollstar* nominated the tour for Most Creative Stage Production for its 2001 awards.

Right after the PopOdyssey Tour wrapped, the tragedy of September 11, 2001, unfolded, which shook up the members of NSYNC like every other American. The band immediately signed on to play a benefit show with other big names of the era at Washington, DC's RFK Stadium, where they'd just recently headlined while on tour. "It's really good to see Rod Stewart fans standing next to 'NSYNC fans standing next to P. Diddy fans," Justin said at one point during the night. "It's good for the country that everybody's ready to rebuild."

It was reported by *Rolling Stone* that the PopOdyssey Tour netted $2.5 million every night, and the guys were finally getting the paychecks they long deserved, enjoying the fruits of their *Celebrity*. As *Rolling Stone* detailed in its feature story in 2001, "The guys are now unbelievably rich and famous and . . . with all the world's opportunities and pleasures on a menu before them."

The writer went on to detail Dolce&Gabbana sneakers, and Justin's collection of 450 pairs of footwear, including every edition of Air Jordans. They had "designer-shredded hand-beaded jeans" and a car fleet including "Dodge Vipers, an Audi TT, a Porsche 911, a BMW M Roadster, a Mercedes, and a Cadillac Escalade with a DVD player, PlayStation 2, and TVs in the headrests." Joey even noted having a *Star Wars*-themed movie theater at home. By this point, the members of NSYNC were also able to buy their families cars and houses, a huge feat for Chris in particular, who recounted to the magazine his years living in poverty.

But fissures started to form. The European leg of the PopOdyssey Tour never came to fruition, and by the time NSYNC hit the road again in 2002 for their final (as of now) tour, dubbed the Celebrity Tour, they were only on the road two months and netted just $33 million, falling behind Paul McCartney, the Rolling Stones, and Cher, and a far cry from the $76 million and $90 million, respectively, of their previous two jaunts.

With openers P. Diddy and Ginuwine, the Celebrity Tour was meant to be a "stripped back" affair that took away the sheen of PopOdyssey and got back to the music, including offering up some Motown and Beatles covers. But there may have been something more to the decision to pull back. Weeks after they got home from the tour, NSYNC went on a "scheduled hiatus"—a time that *Billboard* recounted would be spent allowing the band to pursue outside opportunities: Justin a solo album, JC production projects, Chris a clothing line, and Joey and Lance the chance to work on their film, *On the Line*. They were, for all intents and purposes, officially on a break. A 20-year break.

WHAT THE CRITICS SAID

Celebrity became NSYNC's bittersweet finale, which made it an extra-special album for fans and the band members themselves. But how did the critical reviews of the record (and its accompanying tours) stack up? In addition to the aforementioned praise from *Rolling Stone* and *Slant*, here's what other journalists had to say.

"*NSYNC are undoubtedly one of the best teen pop groups America has ever given us. . . . 2000's *No Strings Attached* raised the pop stakes with its sustained musical brilliance and quite rightly became the fastest selling album of all time. . . . *Celebrity* is pretty damn fine too." —Alex Needham, *NME*

"*NSYNC is self-aware, not just of their position in the pop world, but how to consolidate their strengths while pushing forward. Since time immemorial (or at least since 1987), any pop group rounds up hot producers before making a new record, but *NSYNC has found producers that accentuate different sides of their music . . . but the emergence of Timberlake and Chasez as credible soulful singers and, yes, songwriters, makes it their best album yet, and one of the best of the teen pop boom of 1999–2001 (and, if the first week sales of *Celebrity* are any indication, it will extend even longer)." —Stephen Thomas Erlewine, *AllMusic*

"*Celebrity* may be the consummate teen-pop experience: It has the R&B swipes, the ballads, the grasps at artistic self-expression, and the requisite Europop. On it, 'N Sync are both puppets and puppet masters. Even if it all crumbles (the muted reception to 'Pop' is ominous), they'll go down swinging." —David Browne, *Entertainment Weekly*

"Pop is what 'N Sync do best, and *Celebrity* shines brightest when the group matures enough to forget about its image and focus on the tunes." —J.D. Considine, *Blender*

PART II

BYE BYE BYE

Joey , JC, Lance, and their assistant
Beth Flanagan flip out in Busch Gardens
Tampa Bay in 2001.

10

TAKING TIME OFF

"The break we're on was a conscious move. We all wanted to do it, and we were ready to do it. Performing at stadiums every night for 50,000 fans takes a little out of you. I was 14 when we started, and we've been touring for the last seven years. The time was right; we were all in the same zone."

—Justin talking to the *New York Post* in 2002

Perhaps it was the exhausting overtime put in during the *No Strings Attached* and *Celebrity* eras, but by the time NSYNC wrapped up a nonstop touring cycle in late April 2002, including even performing at a concert for the 2002 Winter Olympics, held in Salt Lake City, they were exhausted. The five guys had been clocking in like workhorses for two years straight, and they need a pause to reset.

What they, along with Jive and manager Johnny Wright, planned on was a temporary respite. Some reports have said it was actually Justin's idea, as he was already in the throes of working on what would become his solo debut *Justified* and needed more time to focus on it. At the time, though, he assumed he could pull double duty: "There's no reason my solo career and *NSYNC can't coexist in the same universe," he'd often said.

Either way, the plan was to take a few vacations, go on a mini-sabbatical, pursue other interests, get their minds off NSYNC for a while, and then come right back to it. They all referred to it as a "scheduled hiatus," starting in May 2002.

NSYNC performs after the medal ceremony at the 2002 Winter Olympic Games in Salt Lake City, Utah.

In fact, when Joey went on *TRL* in mid-April 2002, he told host Carson Daly that, upon the culmination of the Celebrity Tour, they'd take a few months off and "would begin working on new material by December of this year or early 2003." Justin also said as much to *Rolling Stone* in a January 2003 feature shortly after the release of *Justified*, telling the journalist that NSYNC would be going back into the studio that fall.

But, of course, it would be 20 years before there would be any shred of new material, with 2023's "Better Place." So, did they or didn't they break up? NSYNC's super extended "hiatus" has been examined with a fine-toothed comb by fans, media, and even the band members themselves. If you would have asked JC, Joey, Chris, and Lance, they were open to

"taking some time apart" but still very much committed to the band; but if you were to ask Justin, he would have unequivocally affirmed, "We were on a break."

In a 2018 *Huffington Post* article titled "A History Of *NSYNC's Breakup, According To Bandmates Not Named Justin Timberlake," JC, Joey, Chris, and Lance opened up about the split. As the article assures, the remaining four "weren't necessarily ready to say bye, bye, bye when the group called it quits . . . despite personal ventures, most of the members assumed that the break wasn't permanent—that they would reunite, record another album, and tour anew."

What was clear was only that they needed some time off. "You're thinking, 'Okay, we've

The guys perform the national anthem during the Closing Ceremony of the Salt Lake City Winter Olympic Games in February 2002.

done this, we've done this, we've done this. I don't know what else we can do," JC told the outlet, explaining that, in the spring of 2002, other interests started blooming, like fashion (Chris), movies (Joey), astronomy (Lance), studio work (JC), and a solo career (Justin). But it's that last part that became the sticking point.

Over time, it became clear Justin wasn't just briefly stepping back—he was stepping away. In a report in *People* magazine, an unnamed source revealed the band had a pivotal meeting in Miami in 2004 after making a one-off appearance at their yearly Challenge for the Children basketball tournament to support their 501I(3) organization (which has raised over $5 million for charity). In the meeting, Justin told his fellow bandmates, point blank, he was done. "The meeting in Miami was to set a target date (to start recording)," said the source, "and then [Justin] drops the bomb on them . . . Justin said he's not in the mood and doesn't think it will work. He doesn't want any part of it." Apparently, at the time he was already working on his sophomore solo album, *FutureSex/LoveSounds*.

"[The others] are undecided right now [about the future of the band]," the source added. "They aren't really talking to [Justin]. They haven't taken it so well." Another person close to the camp said Chris, JC, Joey, and Lance felt at the time that Justin "strung them along until he was sure his solo career would work."

At best, the reveal "blindsided" some members, while others deemed it a "betrayal."

As Lance explained to the *Dallas Observer* in a preview of his 2007 memoir *Out of Sync*, "When I talk about that time in Miami when Justin told us he didn't want to do it anymore, I wanted people to feel what I felt at that time.

And it did feel like betrayal. I felt heartbroken." In doing press for the book in 2007, he also confirmed the relationship status of NSYNC as a "breakup," telling the *Orlando Sentinel*, "No one did know that answer until recently [but we are] definitely broken up. It's not a hiatus. Justin made it clear that he wouldn't be interested in discussing another album any time soon."

Joey told *Variety* that the way it transpired was a shock to him. "I was not blindsided by [NSYNC's breakup]," Fatone said. "I was more blindsided as far as [Justin] coming out with music and not knowing that he was going to go and do an actual album/tour thing."

Over the ensuing years, Justin has said that the breakup should not have come as a surprise to the other members as he had tried to be candid with the band; he was simply "growing out of [NSYNC]." He even went so far as to tell *Hollywood Reporter* that he felt he "cared more about the music than some of the other people in the group," adding, "I felt like I had other music I wanted to make and that I needed to follow my heart."

The signs were already there, especially if Justin and his team were reading the press and getting ideas. In a March 2002 review of the Celebrity Tour, MTV's Leah Greenblatt asserted, "Justin was quickly established as the star of the show—at least as far as the Jumbotron cameramen were concerned . . . Justin especially reveled in his role, and played the audience like a Stratocaster, goading them into sing-alongs and putting in some quality time alone up front at the lip of the stage." As well, the *New York Times*' Kelefa Sanneh echoed what many had already said about the song "Gone," in which Justin is the leader of the pack (and helped write it), with Kelefa deeming it "the best song the group has ever recorded."

Rumors of Justin's solo album started percolating around the same time. In pre-Grammy 2002 coverage reported on by FOX News that March, writer Roger Friedman was at a Jive Records party and shared, "I was told that he is hard at work on a solo album, which may be more than halfway completed. 'It's going to be huge,' said one music insider who's heard some of the results." In the same night, Justin gave a taste of his solo power, as Roger recalled, "Timberlake, jumped on stage, took the mic, and worked hard to show that he is more than a flash in the pan. He was impressive."

It was no surprise to the rest of NSYNC that Justin would go on to superstardom. "We all knew Justin was going to become a huge solo artist. He's a super-talented guy," Lance told *Dallas Observer*. But what was curious to them was, why was he the only one?

While Chris, Joey, and Lance told *Huffington Post* they didn't really have a desire or "feel pressure" to embark on their own solo careers, as they were tied up in other projects that whet their creative appetites, it didn't make sense to them why JC—who also released a debut single, "Blowin' Me Up (With Her Love)" in 2002 and his one and only solo album, 2004's *Schizophrenic*—wasn't as big as Justin.

"I thought JC's album was going to be just as big as Justin's, but it wasn't," Lance divulged to *Dallas Observer*. Chris added to *Huffington Post*, "It surprises me that JC isn't just as big, because JC is as talented. . . . I really wish JC was out there doing a little more. He still has so much to offer."

Justin himself echoed that sentiment with MTV, saying, "In my opinion, [JC] had the best voice out of all of us. Out of all the boy bands,

call 'em what you will, he was the one that could out-sing all of us."

But there was something else special about Justin that perhaps JC didn't always bring to the table: Justin was magnetizing. If you look at commentary from those outside the band who worked with him, they all tell a story of being transfixed by his voice—and his charisma. As *Entertainment Tonight* reported in 2020 for the twentieth anniversary of *No Strings Attached*, "Timberlake's effervescent energy and eagerness left a strong impression on those who worked with him on the group's sophomore album." Producer Andreas Carlsson recalled, "I remember Justin running in and out, like one of those toys with a [wind-up] screw that keeps going until it runs out. He was jumping up and down going, 'Do you want me to do more? What do you want me to do?' He was like an athlete and . . . worked so hard, striving for perfection."

There's also no doubt that Justin's profile grew as a direct result of his relationship with Britney Spears. The constant coverage of the couple for three years straight, in 1999 and the early 2000s, turned him into a household name, especially as Britney's star wattage grew brighter. It's really no surprise that he used it as leverage in his *Justified* album promo, which was released around the time of the dissolution of the couple's relationship.

Justin was just begging to be called up from the boy band bench into the all-star celebrity lineup, and Johnny Wright knew it. To this day, Johnny continues to manage Justin's solo career as part of his Wright Entertainment Group roster (with help from co-manager Lynn Harless, Justin's mom). The fact that all of those closest to the band seemed to be in on the switch-up was incredibly disheartening to the band.

Chris, Justin, Joey, and JC with Mickey Mouse in 2000.

"It wasn't [just Justin]," Joey astutely asserted to *Variety*. "It was the record company. . . . When you're younger, you think it's that person. But then you look at the whole bigger scheme of things, and you go, 'Oh, that's why I wasn't there for that.' That's the business."

Lance also added that he was thrown by the fact that NSYNC's supporting team was in the know on the Justin developments and

kept the other four guys in the dark: "It's that our whole team, our record label, our management . . . they all knew. They all knew it was over for three years before they told me. . . . I'm sitting there getting ready for a new album as everyone else knows we're moving on."

While Justin's solo career has become a scapegoat for the end of NSYNC, it was just one of many factors that likely would've led to that result. For one, in the post-9/11 world, the frivolity of pop music seemed futile. As *PopMatters* opined at the time, "Had we reached a tipping point where we no longer wanted music that either glorified violence or reveled in shallow materialism?" Pop took a backseat as much of the world looked to meaning and think pieces. Major tours of the day, from the likes of Madonna, Britney Spears, and Janet Jackson, were also canceled as the country tried to reconfigure security measures after the terrorist attacks, putting a sizeable downturn on the whole industry. That may have also been one of the reasons why the early 2002 Celebrity Tour was so stripped back.

Family-friendly entertainment was also a huge seller at the time, as many parents tried to give their kids an escape from the harrowing times. By then, NSYNC were starting to outgrow their Disney roots, as both the band and their fans got older. In their place came ventures like Kidz Bop, kid-friendly versions of popular music of the day, with the first in the series released in October 2001.

As *Entertainment Weekly* reported earlier in 2001, the guys were seen as adults, and it was affecting their image with fans. "Last week millions of teenage hearts shattered when rumors surfaced that 'N Sync singer Joey Fatone and his unnamed longtime girlfriend will become parents early this

Lance, Joey, Justin, JC, and Chris perform in Oakland, California, during the band's Celebrity Tour in 2002.

THE BIGGEST SOLO STARS

Justin may have become one of the biggest solo male recording artists of all time when he split from NSYNC in 2002, but he wasn't the first. Straying from the group has long been a phenomenon in pop music. In fact, *U Discover Music* refers to it as one of the scene's "most enduring rites of passage," adding, "If you're a key member (or even a less-key member) of a successful band, sooner or later the solo bug is going to bite." Here are some of the other big stars who successfully branched out.

Michael Jackson: The singer, who started his career as part of family group the Jackson 5, went solo in the '70s and ultimately became the undisputed King of Pop.

Beyoncé (below): Just a year after Justin went solo, Queen Bey did the same in 2003, taking some time off from Destiny's Child. And the move paid off: to date, she's the most-nominated woman in Grammy history.

Gwen Stefani: All eyes were on Gwen when she fronted No Doubt. Soon enough the "Just A Girl" singer started working on her own music, fashion line, and makeup line, and of course got a seat on *The Voice.*

Harry Styles: Much like Justin, Harry has become arguably the most famous member of boy band One Direction, a development that materialized once he began working on his Grammy-winning solo works and as he heated up Hollywood.

Ricky Martin: Originally a member of Puerto Rican boy band Menudo, a gig he took at the age of twelve, the "Livin' la Vida Loca" singer has gone on to become one of the most recognized Latin singers of all-time with 70 million records sold.

Diana Ross (below)*:* As a member of the Supremes, living legend Diana Ross was part of one of the biggest-selling girl groups of all time. The hits would keep on coming as she moved out on her own in the '70s, with *Billboard* once hailing her as Female Entertainer of the Century.

Paul McCartney: There isn't a more recognized band on the planet than the Beatles, and while each of the four mop tops took a stab at solo careers, Paul McCartney's has been one of the most successful (and most enduring), selling more than 100 million albums.

JC celebrates the launch of *Schizophrenic* in New York in March 2004.

topical lyrical fury. The late '90s brought a wave of nu metal bands like Korn, Slipknot, and Limp Bizkit, who were tearing up the charts. By 2001, contemporaries Linkin Park had the best-selling album of the year with *Hybrid Theory*, claiming the top spot while NSYNC's *Celebrity* came in at No. 3. By 2004, MTV reported that pop punk was also a factor to contend with: "The notion of 'boy bands' has changed tremendously, as young audiences find their heartthrobs not among pop groups but rather in the ranks of groups like Good Charlotte, Yellowcard, and New Found Glory."

The way music was consumed was also changing. As mentioned previously, Napster reared its ugly head in the early 2000s just as the digital revolution was beginning its ascent. On October 23, 2001, the first edition of Apple's holy grail, the iPod, was released, changing the course of music for all history as mp3 files became king. There was no more camping out at record stores or buying multiple copies of an album, now everything was done behind a screen—and artists were lucky if they got paid for streams.

All of it begs the question, if NSYNC had, perhaps, come back in December 2003 to record a new album, as Joey theorized prematurely to *TRL*, would they have even been able to continue? Or was the unintended breakup actually a smart move?

On Reddit, a conversation about the manner in which NSYNC parted ways heated up again in the fall of 2023, just as the guys were coming back into the fold. The question was posed: "How do we think fans would have reacted if *NSYNC had broken up properly instead of leaving us (and themselves!) in limbo with an indefinite hiatus?" User StarScarlet responded, "Personally an announcement would have

summer," the magazine reported, adding, "But will his plan to croon lullabies make teen fans say bye, bye, bye?"

Music tastes were changing too. Like most other boy bands, NSYNC had a discernable shelf life, their popularity fading as kids became teens and young adults and found music that spoke to the frustration of their early adulthood. At the dawn of the new millennium, nu metal was having a big moment; the rap-metal mashup genre was a 180 from pop music, driven by aggressive beats, heavy riffs, and been better. It would have given us all closure instead of the broken promises that we got. I understand Justin's first album blew up, but a nice announcement right after the success would have been a better move."

Another Redditor, _Judas_, opined, "I think not announcing the breakup was a business decision meant to favor Justin's solo career. You could tell by the time 'Pop' came out that the energy was gone and it was more or less a place holder for greater things. . . . 'Gone' was an obvious soft launch and even then it felt kind of slimy to watch the rest of Nsync play backup singer." Some even theorized that, had NSYNC formalized their breakup, it would have given JC a better chance at his solo career, and others admitted they now have "abandonment issues for life."

Even with the band on a break, the individual members didn't go quietly into the night, remaining in the headlines for decades to come. And, right after the "scheduled hiatus" began, the five re-banded for two key events

in 2003 and 2004 that gave fans a glimmer of (wasted) hope.

At the 45th annual Grammy Awards in 2003, NSYNC took the stage to offer a tribute to the Bee Gees, just a month after Maurice Gibb, one of the founding members of the disco pop group, passed away. For it, NSYNC returned to their roots as an a cappella group with a tender medley (and Justin's beatboxing). The group received a standing ovation; it would be their final televised performance together for ten years.

In 2004, the five also made a one-off appearance at their yearly Challenge for the Children basketball tournament, singing the national anthem. Even then, they skirted around questions about getting back together.

"You caught us on the wrong day," JC tersely told MTV. "If you would have caught us [tomorrow] we would have had a better answer for you." Justin added, "We're going to enjoy the weekend, and as Monday rolls around, we'll get to the business stuff and we'll go from there."

The digital edition of Britney Spears's 2023 memoir, *The Woman in Me*.

JUSTIN BECOMES A JUSTIFIED SUPERSTAR

"I turned on *TRL* the other day, and I'm the old guy now. Avril Lavigne and B2K, they're the new little faces of teen pop . . . I'm somewhere in the middle, starting from zero, rebuilding my whole base. This year has been all about change. Big change. I ended a four-year relationship. I bought a house in LA. I embarked on a solo career. And, on top of that, I did it all in front of the world, without losing my head."

—Justin Timberlake talking to *Rolling Stone* in 2003

Suffice to say, Justin has come a long way from *Star Search* and Mouseketeering. Now in his forties, you could devote an entire book to analyzing his solo career alone—a career that has produced six albums and 88 million units sold, plus 39 Grammy nominations and 10 awards won. All those

Justin performs at Nassau Coliseum in Uniondale, New York, in August 2003.

benchmarks best even NSYNC, who had just four records and sales of 70 million total.

In addition to his Grammy nominations and wins, Justin has received four Emmy Awards, nine *Billboard* Music Awards, MTV's Michael Jackson Video Vanguard Award, and iHeart Radio's Innovator Award. He was also a recipient of an Academy Award nomination for "Can't Stop The Feeling!" in 2016, the song he contributed to the first *Trolls* soundtrack, and was inducted into the Memphis Music Hall of Fame. He also holds an honorary doctorate from Berklee College of Music. After those seven years with NSYNC, Justin finally got the credibility he long craved as an artist.

Justin has also been a "force on the *Billboard* charts" since going solo, says the magazine, and is "one of the biggest stars of his generation" according to *Grammy.com.* *Rolling Stone* even hailed him as the "new King of Pop," a cloying definition that pits JT against one of his biggest idols, Michael Jackson. With his incredible success and career highs—which have also included countless collaborations and acting gigs and accolades—Justin is considered one of the biggest male solo artists of all time. And to think it all started with the bold move in 2002 to break away from the very group that made him.

Justin has always been the baby of the group, so you could say time was on his side when he dipped out of NSYNC. At the time, he was just twenty-one years old, while some of the guys were pushing thirty (or already in their thirties). Justin also said that making his own music had long been a goal. "When I was ten years old, my dream was to have my own record," the singer told Apple Music's Zane Lowe. And the time to do so just seemed right after NSYNC's fourth and, to date, final album *Celebrity* in 2001.

Justin at the album release party for his solo debut, *Justified*, in 2002.

"I would wake up every morning feeling this more and more of an urge to step out on my own and try my own hand as a musician just by myself," Justin revealed to Oprah Winfrey in an intimate MasterClass conversation in 2014, though he ultimately conceded he was torn about closing the door on that huge chapter in his life. "It's one of the best/worst things that I have ever done. It was bittersweet. It was hard to say goodbye to that era . . . all around me [were people saying], 'Why wouldn't you ride this out? You're the biggest group in the world. Why would you walk away from this?' . . . But I felt it changing. I felt music changing. And I felt myself changing."

That shift is felt all over *Justified*, Justin's debut solo album. It was released on NSYNC's label Jive to much fanfare on November 5, 2002, just six months after NSYNC announced their hiatus and shortly after Justin broke things off with Britney, leading some to deem the effort a "breakup album." *Justified* was created in just six weeks with the help of lead producers the Neptunes (returning after their work on *Celebrity)* and Timbaland.

But if it seems like a rushed affair, none of that translated to the final product, which elevated Justin into more mature territory. Of course, his vocals were still the primary focus, but the music took away the innocence of teen pop and replaced it with a funky backbeat, rhythm and blues standards, and hip-hop swagger that called to mind all the greats: Prince, Stevie Wonder, and Michael Jackson. MTV hailed it as "a broad, ambitious step from the clean, blissful pop of 'NSYNC," and *Grammy.com* opined, "the 13-track LP delved into the singer's R&B and old-school influences, artistically re-introducing himself

while laying the groundwork for the global solo stardom to come."

Justin recounted to *Billboard*, "I was trying to make a multi-dimensional record; a record that captured the vibe of my favorite time in music, the '60s. . . . I got to live in my own musical dream world and play a little hip-hop, a little old-school R&B, a little classic rock. It was so much fun—and I learned a lot about making music in a totally different way than I was used to."

Justin with the Neptunes at the 2003 MTV Video Music Awards.

Justin with Jimmy Fallon in a 2024 episode for *Saturday Night Live*.

Interestingly enough, as with "Gone," the music on *Justified* was first written largely by the Neptunes' Pharrell Williams and Chad Hugo to present to Michael Jackson for consideration, but when he passed, it opened the tracks up to become Justin's first shot at solo gold.

Justified produced five singles: the debut "Like I Love You," which hit No. 11 on the *Billboard Hot 100* and spent 20 total weeks on the chart; "Cry Me a River," and "Rock Your Body," which shot up to the No. 3 and No. 5 spots on *Billboard*, respectively, and each spent about 20–22 weeks on the chart; as well as "Senorita," which reached No. 27, and "Still On My Brain," which didn't end up charting.

Justified has been certified 3x Platinum by the Recording Industry Association of America® for sales of 3 million units. The album also peaked at the No. 2 position on the *Billboard 200* chart and spent 84 weeks in the rankings. It was also nominated for a number of awards at the 46th annual Grammys, winning Best Pop Vocal Album and Best Male Pop Vocal Performance for the song "Cry Me a River," providing Justin's first-ever wins from the Recording Academy.

Justin himself thought *Justified* was some of his best work. As he boldly told *Rolling Stone*, "I've had some of the greatest experiences with [JC, Chris, Lance, and Joey], but do I think that what I've done with [*Justified*] is ten times better than anything 'Nsync has ever done? Yes, I do. But I'm a cocky bastard."

When it came to the promotional cycle, it felt very much like the old days, with Justin, his mug, and his moves *everywhere*. He took over *TRL*; landed on the 2002 MTV VMAs, where he won three awards and his performance— for better or worse—drew Michael Jackson copycat claims; he appeared on the 2002 *Billboard* Music Awards; hosted *Saturday Night Live* for the first time in 2003 (where his skits spoofing a Barry Gibb talk show and appearing as Jessica Simpson in drag showed natural acting chops and propelled him on to more gigs); sat down with Barbara Walters for an interview; appeared on covers and centerfolds of magazines from *Rolling Stone* to *Entertainment Weekly*; took over the McDonald's "I'm Lovin' It" campaign; and hit the road with former *Mickey Mouse Club* classmate Christina Aguilera on the Justified & Stripped Tour in the summer of 2003.

While everything seemed positive for the burgeoning superstar, some controversy did ignite, particularly when it came to the women in his orbit. Janet Jackson appeared on the track "(And She Said) Take Me Now," which sexualized the female character in the song. The collaboration (and the same manager) led to the duo's joint appearance at the Super Bowl Halftime Show in 2004, with the wardrobe malfunction seen 'round the world, which Janet unfairly bore the brunt of (see sidebar).

And then there was the video for "Cry Me a River," which featured Justin as a jilted ex-lover who seeks revenge on a former, cheating flame by breaking into her house and filming a sex video with a new partner. The ex in the video looked a hell of a lot like Britney Spears, down to her trademark newsboy cap and

tattoo, and was considered by some to be retribution for allegations of real-life infidelity. The video was racy, raunchy, and rather creepy; it all but assured Justin was no more interested in the child's play of a boy band and had matured into sex symbol status. The backlash to the video was swift, with many pointing out the obvious comparisons and calling it a publicity stunt.

"I didn't make this video so I could sit around and talk about it," Justin said to *Rolling Stone*, attempting to defend himself. "It's a video, and when you watch it, either you have a sense of humor or you don't. [The girl] doesn't represent anybody. She represents a female in the storyline. I haven't gone public about my relationship." To this day, Justin continues to include the hit in his live set list, and in recent years, has become defensive about the track, especially around the release of Britney's late 2023 memoir, *The Woman In Me*.

In January 2024, when playing an intimate New York club gig to drum up excitement for his sixth studio album, *Everything I Thought It Was*, Justin introduced the song with the statement, "I'd like to take this opportunity to apologize to absolutely fucking nobody." Per *People*, Britney clapped back on her private Instagram account, sharing, "Someone told me someone was talking shit about me on the streets !!! [sic]. . . . Do you want to bring it to the court or will you go home crying to your mom like you did last time??? I'm not sorry !!!"

Even so, the video criticism didn't make a dent in the impact Justin had on early 2000s culture, and his love life was anything but muted or forgotten. At the time, Justin had high-profile relationships with Cameron Diaz and Spice Girl Emma Bunton, the former causing a paparazzi race. In the 2003 *Rolling*

Stone feature, Justin also plays coy about trysts with Alyssa Milano and even Janet Jackson and admits to crushing on Shania Twain and Natalie Imbruglia.

By 2012, he had settled down with wife Jessica Biel; the couple now has two sons, Silas and Phineas. Fatherhood was on his mind in a *Hollywood Reporter* interview, in which he ponders about his children following in his footsteps. "Would I want my child to follow my path? You know, I haven't been able to answer that question in my mind," he said. "If he wanted it bad enough, I suppose I could teach him a lot about what not to do."

Not that it's been half-bad. After the pop culture maelstrom of *Justified*, Justin went on to make several more hit records, including *FutureSex/LoveSounds* in 2006, which hit No. 1 on the *Billboard 200* when it debuted and spent 106 weeks on the chart. The album was bolstered by the strength of singles "SexyBack" (featuring Timbaland), "My Love" (featuring T.I.), and "What Goes Around . . . Comes Around." Black Eyed Peas' will.i.am also guests on "Damn Girl."

After a long musical gap in which Justin turned his focus on acting, he came back strong with parts one and two of *The 20/20 Experience* in 2013. In version one, Jay-Z guests on "Suit & Tie"; for take two, "Take Back The Night" became a bona fide hit, and guest stars included Drake on "Cabaret" and a repeat Jay-Z on "Murder" (Jay-Z and JT would also go on tour together that summer). Both albums debuted at No. 1 on the *Billboard 200*.

In 2018 came *Man of the Woods*, which again featured his go-to production team of the Neptunes and Timbaland and had well-received guest spots from Alicia Keys on "Morning Light" and Chris Stapleton on "Say Something."

That album also debuted at No. 1 on the *Billboard 200*.

In 2024, Justin was busy promoting his sixth album, *Everything I Thought It Was* (which came out March 15 that year) and the first single, "Selfish" (curiously, also the title of an NSYNC song on *Celebrity* and a song by Britney). That January, the promotion cycle brought him back to *Saturday Night Live* as a music guest and had him reunite with *SNL* sparring partner and good friend Jimmy Fallon on his late-night show to spill the beans on the album and accompanying tour. The 2024 Forget Tomorrow World Tour was Justin's first in five years and brought the superstar back to the arenas he was accustomed to playing, with many dates sold out.

Justin's vast music catalog also includes a number of top-tier collaborations and writing contributions, such as several tracks on Jay-Z's *Magna Carta . . . Holy Grail* album, the song "4 Minutes" with Madonna, "Ayo Technology" with 50 Cent, Nelly's "Work It," "The Other Side" with SZA, "Where Is the Love?" and "My Style" with the Black Eyed Peas, "Signs" with Snoop Dogg, Duran Duran's "Nite Runner" and "Falling Down," Ciara's "Love Sex Magic," Michael Jackson's posthumous song "Love Never Felt So Good," and of course the comical "Dick In A Box" with Lonely Island, which went on to find cultural infamy. For a time, Justin also had his own record label, Tennman Records, in partnership with Interscope.

His filmography is just as extensive, with Justin somehow finding the time to tag team on his two creative pursuits throughout the last two decades. Some of his most notable roles include playing Napster founder Sean Parker in *The Social Network*, starring in sci-fi caper

Justin with his wife, Jessica Biel, at the 2024 Vanity Fair Oscar Party.

In Time, Woody Allen's 1950s period piece *Wonder Wheel*, rom-coms including *Friends with Benefits* and *Bad Teacher,* and voiceover work in the *Trolls* franchise.

In 2022, it was reported by *Variety* that Justin had sold his song catalog to Hipgnosis Song Management for an estimated $100 million (a much better money move than when he forked over $35 million for a share of MySpace in 2011). In a statement, Hipgnosis CEO Merck Mercuriadis said, "Justin Timberlake is not only one of the most influential artists of the last 20 years but he's also one of the greatest songwriters of all time."

SUPER BOWL CONTROVERSY

The first time Justin appeared at the Super Bowl Halftime Show with NSYNC in 2001 was a smashing success, as the boy band teamed up with Aerosmith for a crossover bonanza that made positive headlines. A few years later, Justin's return to the field with Janet Jackson in 2004 became a PR nightmare.

Not only did he receive criticism for not inviting his NSYNC bandmates to be part of the performance, but during the *Justified* song "Rock Your Body," things went "awry," as Janet later told CNN. As Justin sang one particular line, he pulled off a part of Janet's stage outfit, which exposed her bare breast, much to the shock of the 140 million people tuned into the telecast. The Federal Communications Commission immediately announced an investigation of the incident. MTV, who helped produce the segment, and CBS both issued apologies.

As did Janet. Her spokesperson, Stephen Huvane, assured CNN it was not intentional and "was a malfunction of the wardrobe." As he clarified, "[Justin] was supposed to pull away the bustier and leave the red-lace bra."

Justin issued an immediate statement, as well, saying, "I am sorry if anyone was offended by the

wardrobe malfunction during the halftime performance at the Super Bowl. It was not intentional and is regrettable." He otherwise tried to stay out of the conversation in the aftermath following the hysteria.

Critics have accused him of letting Janet Jackson take more of the blame, which undoubtedly affected her career and the promotion of her 2004 album *Damita Jo*. In the years since, particularly after the 2021 Hulu documentary *Framing Britney Spears* brought into question some of Justin's former missteps, he has issued apologies.

"I have seen the messages, tags, comments, and concerns and I want to respond. I am deeply sorry for the times in my life where my actions contributed to the problem, where I spoke out of turn, or did not speak up for what was right," Timberlake posted to Instagram, as reported by *USA Today*. He apologized to Janet Jackson and Britney Spears, and went on to say, "The industry is flawed. It sets men, especially white men, up for success. As a man in a privileged position I have to be vocal about this. Because of my ignorance, I didn't recognize it for all that it was while it was happening in my own life but I do not want to ever benefit from others being pulled down again."

JC GETS A
NEW "CREW"

"As Justin goes out and does his solo thing, he's making new fans he wouldn't have had as 'N Sync. Hopefully I'll be doing that as well. And so maybe people will be more open-minded when we get back together."

—JC talking to the *New York Times* in late 2003, ahead of the release of his debut solo album

JC has often been described as having the best voice out of all the members of NSYNC—and the best voice of all modern boy band members, for that matter. "He could out-sing all of us," Justin once told MTV. He was also the second most active member of the band, after Justin, when it came to writing songs on *No Strings Attached* and *Celebrity* and singing lead.

So, it was no surprise when he started to work on his own music, around the same time Justin was pursuing solo endeavors. JC's first take was the single "Blowin' Me Up (With Her Love)," an upbeat pop number with heart and a beat, coming together in a mid-song breakdown that just begs people to get up and move.

The song appeared on the soundtrack for the 2002 teen flick *Drumline* and combined notes of Prince, Michael Jackson, and George Michael; it peaked at No. 35 on the *Billboard Hot 100* chart. The movie was based on music producer Dallas Austin's real-life experiences in a high school marching band (with the love interest storyline based on P. Diddy's former flame Kim Porter, whom Dallas Austin dated at a young age). Dallas produced both the film and the soundtrack, and told MTV at the time that he had recorded four tracks with JC. "We've been doing some great, great material. At first, he wasn't going to do a record, but I think now he's kind of interested, so we'll probably just keep

JC performs during the Y100 Jingle Ball 2003 at Office Depot Center in Fort Lauderdale, Florida.

recording," Dallas said. "We were just writing songs for the movie and we caught a niche and it was like, 'Oh shit, this is cool for you, let's keep going.'"

To Dallas's point, working on the track inspired JC to formalize his solo plans. Before getting the call from the producer to pen a song for the soundtrack, JC wasn't all that interested in taking a solo career seriously.

"We'd been running for seven years straight on the road, and the first thing I thought was: vacation. I have other best friends besides the guys in 'N Sync, and they get neglected. So I settled down and chilled out and did a bunch of nothing with them," JC told the *New York Times* of his initial plans during NSYNC's hiatus. But, after working with Dallas and presenting the "Blowin' Me Up" single to the head honchos at his label, Jive Records, both parties insisted JC start working on a full-length record.

"I said, '[Justin] is doing his thing; I just want to chill,'" he recalled to the *New York Times*. "Then Dallas sat down with me and said, 'Why aren't you doing a record?' I said, 'I was just getting used to living again.'"

It took two years, but JC's solo debut *Schizophrenic* did finally come out in February 2004. "The problem is my timetable caught up to me," JC explained to MTV of the delay in putting out the album. Originally intended for release in summer 2003, it had been pushed back several times.

To help package it, JC enlisted the help of Dallas Austin as well as former NSYNC producer Alex Greggs and former *Mickey Mouse Club* castmate Tony Lucca. English electro duo Basement Jaxx also helped pen the rollicking number, "Shake It."

JC sings during an NSYNC concert, as part of their 2002 Celebrity Tour.

MUSICAL MAN

Like Joey's ambitions for Broadway (more on that in the next chapter), JC also wanted to try staged musicals. In 2014, JC was tied to a new all-star touring cast of Andrew Lloyd Webber and Tim Rice's *Jesus Christ Superstar,* in which he was supposed to play Pontius Pilate. The rest of the ensemble behind the production, which was slated to visit American arenas like Madison Square Garden, also included other big music stars like Destiny's Child's Michelle Williams, Incubus' Brandon Boyd, and punk legend John Lydon (Johnny Rotten from the Sex Pistols).

JC was excited at the opportunity, telling the *Tampa Bay Times,* "We've been going through each scene almost line by line and talking about, what is the motivation here? . . . I've been working with the director first to establish who this person is, and then put the life into his body, and then allow that kind of body and attitude to lend itself to developing the way this person would sound singing."

Unfortunately, poor ticket sales ultimately doomed the production and it was canceled before it could really take off. Still, JC was inspired by the experience and, in recent years, has started working on developing his own musicals, as he revealed on Lance's *Frosted Tips* podcast.

"There are similarities [between writing a pop hit and musical theater songs] and there are some very big differences," he shared with *Billboard* in 2023. "When you're working on a musical, there's always a bigger picture and the story is always the driving force. . . . What really attracted me to it lately is that there's such a human experience in live theater. There's no hiding. There's no AI up there. There's no dirty tricks. It's people up there giving you everything in that moment."

The record was far more expansive—and expressive—than anything NSYNC had done, with influences ranging from Donna Summer-era disco (her huge hit "I Feel Love" is sampled in one track) to Stevie Wonder-esque funky R&B with soul, electronica, reggae, new wave, and club notes mixed in. Most songs were either veiled inuendoes or overt admissions about sex, with "Some Girls (Dance With Women)," "One Night Stand," and "All Day Long I Dream About Sex" being prime examples. In fact, JC remembered execs at Jive telling him, "You know you're going to scare a few moms with this music."

Yet, "it had to be fun," JC told *The Sunday Times* of his intention with the album. "There was no point otherwise. I'm not one of those people who needs to be famous and I don't need the money." *Schizophrenic* was also his chance to break out of the boy band bubble that had been erected around him the past nearly decade. ''People are used to us maybe catering to a pop crowd that's maybe all girls, but I didn't make my record for any specific audience or do any compromising," he told the *New York Times*.

While critics largely approved of the album—which was called "an ambitious, creative, and highly enjoyable endeavor" by *PopMatters*—the promotion didn't go exactly as planned. First, JC had to contend with criticism of the album cover art, which depicted the singer in a straightjacket. Many mental health advocacy groups accused the artist of continuing to encourage stigmas. "I apologize to anyone I may have offended with the title and cover of my album," JC said in a statement. "I am truly sorry if I've upset anyone." He has clarified in interviews that the title and theme were meant to represent the many musical styles he wanted to incorporate into the tracks.

JC at the launch of his debut solo album in 2004.

There was another hiccup during the album's release month, in February 2004. JC was booked to play the NFL Pro Bowl in Hawaii just a week after the 2004 Super Bowl, but given the controversy around Justin and Janet's shenanigans, and with the overt lyrics in JC's solo material, he was yanked from the performance by producers who feared more FCC fines. It was a huge blow to both album exposure and reminding former and would-be fans that he had new material. Thankfully, a short order of tour dates helped somewhat, particularly in the UK, where JC was booked to support Britney Spears on her Onyx Hotel Tour.

In reviews, JC was hailed as "crossing the line from sheer musician to pure entertainer . . . [and] setting out to produce The Greatest Show on Earth" (*PopMatters*), though in the same

ABOVE: JC walks the
red carpet at the 2005
MTV Movie Awards.

OPPOSITE: JC performs
during a show at the
House of Blues in
West Hollywood in
November 2002.

review, the writer admitted, "discussing Chasez on his own merit is a difficult task indeed."

There were so many factors working against him, not the least of which was the fact that JC seemed, for all intents and purposes, to be working in the shadow of Justin. The unfortunate delays of *Schizophrenic* put him two years behind JT's rising star. "The problem is that boy bands rarely spawn more than one successful solo member," noted *The Sunday Times,* and this belief seemed to plague JC from the onset of his solo career. Unlike Justin's albums, nearly all of which would claim the No. 1 spot on the *Billboard 200* charts upon release, JC's *Schizophrenic* peaked at No. 17 and only spent four weeks on the chart in total. It was a dismal debut.

"JC had all the essentials for becoming a successful pop star just like Justin, but poor

marketing, overtly sexual lyrics, a debut album that tried to accomplish too much, and overall bad timing didn't take him down that path," said *Billboard.*

By 2005, JC told interviewers that he was working on the follow-up to *Schizophrenic,* under the working title *The Story of Kate.* He teased it to MTV, noting that lauded producer Timbaland was helping steer the direction. "This one is going to be a little more pop-alternative," he added. "The last one had a pretty broad spectrum, so this time I'm gonna give people more of a journey in the same direction."

As time ticked by, and no record was released, some started to wonder if it would ever see the light of day. By 2007, JC followed up on the progress with MTV, sharing that Justin was even in the studio with him helping

to write some songs. "Justin has got more groove than just about anybody out there, so there is a great combination when the two of us get together in the studio," he said, noting the songwriting duo penned tracks called "Until Yesterday" and "God Bless America."

"Until Yesterday" was released in late 2006 as a digital single, but by that time, the momentum was gone. *The Story of Kate* was shelved as Jive dropped JC in 2007. Afterward, JC changed course and started working behind the boards, developing material for other artists, including Matthew Morrison (of *Glee* fame), *American Idol* alum David Archuleta, and even Backstreet Boys' AJ McLean (JC wrote two songs for AJ's 2011 album *Have It All*).

As 2008 rolled around, JC found a new "crew," teaming up with *American Idol's* Randy Jackson to help judge a new MTV reality show called *Randy Jackson Presents: America's Best Dance Crew*, which sought to discover those with the best moves across the country and became a launchpad for dance crews like Jabbawockeez.

"When we made this show, I did it because I believed in it. I liked the fact that this is people that are of the street level, that have aspirations for people to see the craft that they do. And so I was all in because the first thing I ever did was dance in public at a competition," JC told *The Hollywood Reporter* in 2012. "And it turns out that there's just no shortage of upcoming talent." JC stayed on as judge for seven seasons (2008–2012) before the series was canceled by

MTV; a short-lived reboot came in 2015, though JC was not attached to the new iteration.

In the years since, JC has remained relatively under the radar. He is also the one member of NSYNC not to marry, though, in the past, he's been linked to actress Eva Longoria and is currently dating his longtime girlfriend, Jennifer HuYoung.

Outside music, JC has had brief acting cameos on shows like *Ghost Whisperer* and *Las Vegas* and appeared as himself on *All That* and *Britain's Next Top Model* as well as in the comedic movie *Opening Night*. In 2023, he teamed up with Meow Mix for a new commercial, helping reimagine the pet food brand's long-running jingle as a boy band hit.

But the singer's sizzle to fizzle journey has been something that fans and even bandmates agree is just wrong. Online, there's a "Justice for JC" campaign, with @justice4jc racking up 142,000 followers and 6.5 million likes on TikTok as of publication; it's devoted to "giving JC from *NSYNC the credit & recognition he DESERVES."

JC knows of the campaign, having acknowledged its existence to *Billboard*, while his NSYNC bandmate Chris admits he's fully behind the push too. "I beg him, like, I would love to hear a record from him," Chris has told *Page Six,* adding, "I don't know if there was a bad taste in his mouth from his first record or what, but I know that there's a bad taste in his mouth from something, and he just won't put it out no matter what . . . He'll do it when he's ready."

In Sync with NSYNC

One of my friends gifted me this binder of handwritten pages that were clearly NSYNC fan fiction. It was told from the first-person perspective, and it was written by someone who picked Joey Fatone as the object of their affection. The writing in the binder began in what I joke was "*in medias res*"—as in, in the middle of the action, and after many, many pages, it left the audience hanging. The narrator was supposedly Joey's childhood friend and girlfriend, named Kelly, who was touring with Joey and the rest of the band. Touchstones include 9–11 (!), becoming pregnant with Joey's baby and then losing the baby, fighting off Joey's ex (also named Kelly?!), and meeting random luminaries such as Marc Blucas (Riley Finn on *Buffy the Vampire Slayer*) and John Rzeznik from the Goo Goo Dolls.

My friend Sacha Mullin and I decided to turn it into a podcast where we chronologically read aloud pages from the binder. We questioned the author's grammatical choices, enjoyed irrelevant notes in the margins, and went on many tangents. Mostly we theorized who we thought the author might be and how old they were (seeing as how it read like a preteen's version of what they thought adulthood was). All the while Sacha accompanied us on his keyboard while we read it like it was an old-fashioned radio play. We never read ahead so the plot twists were just as much a surprise to us as it was to our audience. This was worth doing for the laughs alone. You can listen to it at https://rayofblight.podbean.com/

Liz Mason, producer and co-host of
***The Found *NSYNC Fan Fiction* Radio Hour**

13

JOEY FINDS THE GREAT WHITE WAY

"I always just loved entertaining and performing. After *NSYNC, there was a sense of, what do you do? I did take a break for a little, then after a while, I was, like, I have to do something!"

—Joey talking to *Variety* in 2018

Joey has always been the ham, the funny guy, the uber-extrovert of the group—and that personality characteristic parlayed well into his burgeoning career in Hollywood and on Broadway during NSYNC's hiatus years. In fact, with roles in the *My Big Fat Greek Wedding* franchise and crime capers like *The Cooler*, plus roles on shows like *Hannah Montana*, hosting gigs on a number of television game shows, and theater runs in *Rent* and *Little Shop of Horrors*, among others, Joey remains the member of NSYNC most in the public eye (besides Justin).

Joey's first real taste of the silver screen came with the 2001 film *On the Line*, the rom-com in which he starred with his boy band brother Lance. It was filmed in the short interim between NSYNC's No Strings Attached Tour and starting work on *Celebrity*. Joey and Lance had been trying their hands at getting a movie in the works for a while, first trying to nab the rights to make *Grease 3* and then, when that didn't happen, pressing the full NSYNC band to make a different kind of movie that would

Joey at curtain call at *Rent* in August 2002.

be a group effort, in the vein of the Beatles' *A Hard Day's Night* or *Spice World*.

Not everyone was interested, so Joey and Lance pressed on with *On the Line*, the inaugural project of Lance's newly formed A Happy Place Productions. He hoped it was the right move, but admitted in an interview with MTV that it was a "huge risk." Still, "I think if you had all five guys of 'NSYNC, people really wouldn't take the movie seriously. This way, there's a couple of us in it, and it's a real movie," he said. "It really stands up on its own." Chris also had a bit part in it and the soundtrack included a few unreleased cuts from NSYNC. It barely grossed $5 million and got sour reviews, which Lance partly blamed on the fact that the movie came out one week after the September 11 attacks, which he believed doomed it to fail.

However, when talking about the film to *Variety*, Joey said, "Me and Lance had a lot of fun. It was our first time doing something outside of *NSYNC, and kind of got us bitten by the little bug as far as producing and wanting to do more films. It was definitely a learning experience."

Shortly thereafter, Joey booked his next big gig, appearing in the 2002 film, *My Big Fat Greek Wedding*, in which he plays Angelo, the gregarious cousin of the main character, Toula, played by actress and the movie's creator Nia Vardalos. Joey filmed his scenes concurrent with working in the studio with NSYNC on *Celebrity*. "We are supportive of anything that anybody else does in the group," he told MTV at the time. "They were able to work the schedule where it was like I flew in [to Toronto] to shoot some of the scenes, then flew back to record."

It's a role Joey went on to return to in both *Greek* sequels. The third installment, which came out in September 2023, was largely

Joey (far right) and Lance (second from right) in *On the Line* (2001).

Joey in *My Big Fat Greek Wedding* (2002).

panned by film critics, although Joey received goodhearted reviews. Says *Variety*, "Angelo (Joey Fatone) and Nikki (Gia Carides) are a breath of fresh air, saving the day in more ways than one, both rescuing their cousins from impending disappointment, and us [the viewers] from a plateau in energy."

Then, Broadway came calling. In the summer of 2002, it was announced that Joey would make his debut in a new production of Jonathan Larson's *Rent* at the Nederlander Theatre in New York. The gig spanned four months, from August to December 2002. He took on the character of Mark, who *Playbill* describes as, "the struggling artist who captures the events of his friends' lives on video." Sound familiar? Joey was already well-versed in that role, being the erstwhile documentarian for NSYNC during their heyday.

In an interview with the *New York Times*, Joey shared that the invite to be on Broadway was, for him, "cutting-edge . . . It's nice to have a chance to play a character, not just be myself." In fact, Joey shared that he had dreamed of doing Broadway since he was involved in music theater in high school. Finally fulfilling the desire was a full-circle moment.

Rent producers also had a motive for casting Joey: bringing in a new audience. As showrunner Jefferey Seller told *Playbill*, "Hopefully, Joey is going to bring in tens of thousands of new audience members who I believe will be converted to *Rent*-heads, who will keep us going for the next couple years."

MTV caught up with a few theatregoers who saw Joey's debut in the production that August and—whether they were NSYNC fans or not—they had rave reviews. "It's more mature, I liked it a lot better than his kiddie concerts," said one fan named Kate. Another named Andrea added, "I was actually really impressed with Joey . . . he pulled it off. I just think that this is different than 'NSYNC, and maybe it'll convert a few 'NSYNC fans, which is cool because this is really an eye-opening play."

A *Rent* devotee named Krista also said, "I can't even count all the guys I've seen play Mark. And honestly, Joey is probably

the second best I've seen, compared to the original. He was really, really natural on stage, and for this being his first show was phenomenal. Usually Justin and JC are the singers in the band, and you don't hear that much from Joey, which is unfortunate, because he can really sing."

Joey apparently even threw some of the dance moves from NSYNC's "Pop" video into his performance. He admitted to MTV that, while he enjoyed being in the musical, it was "a lot of work," and very different from the demands of being in a boy band. "You do eight shows a week, that's what I'm doing [with

Rent]. Usually [with NSYNC], I'm doing five or six shows a week with two days off. Here you only have one day off, and you do four shows over the weekend for matinees, so it's going to be interesting on my voice."

The hard work paid off, though, as Joey got several additional offers to appear in Broadway productions once *Rent* wrapped. In 2004, he joined a reprisal of *Little Shop of Horrors* in the lead role of Seymour; in 2013, he was cast as Bert in *42nd Street* for the Pittsburgh's Civic Light Opera summer season; and later years brought roles in productions of *The Producers* and *Rock of Ages*.

Joey soon also started accumulating film and TV opportunities. Joey's IMDb page is extensive, with more than 60 acting credits to his name. In addition to the films mentioned above, there were spots in *Homie Spumoni* in 2006, *The Bros.* in 2007, and *Beethoven's Big Break*

in 2008. Joey also appeared in a number of animated and/or kids shows including voiceover work on *Kim Possible, Robot Chicken,* and *JoJo's Circus* from 2004–2009. Then, in 2017, Joey teamed up with fellow boy band alum Joey McIntyre from New Kids On The Block for the latter's Pop TV series, *Return of the Mac.* Joey also had some acting roles in horror films like 2011 flick *Inkubus* and 2016's *Dead 7*, which was a "post-apocalyptic zombie horror western film" written by none other than Nick Carter.

Another big break came in 2007, when Joey was tapped for the fourth season of uber-popular reality competition series *Dancing with the Stars*. He and pro partner Kym Johnson came in second place, losing out to Olympian Apolo Anton Ohno. As Joey later remarked to *Variety*, he was initially puzzled at the offer to be part of the show: "I was like, why would anybody want to see me dance?

Joey and Jessica Snow Wilson during closing night of *Little Shop of Horrors* on Broadway in 2004.

But they were persistent and I agreed." Though, he shouldn't have been taken aback; after all, one of his key responsibilities as a member of a boy band was mastering choreography. It's the same reason why Lance, Backstreet Boys' Nick Carter and AJ McLean, and NKOTB's Joey McIntyre had appeared on *Dancing with the Stars* in previous seasons.

Joey has also played host for a number of reality and competition franchises over the years, including NBC/CMT's *The Singing Bee,* the long-running game show *Family Feud, Rewrapped* on the Food Network, *Common Knowledge* on the Game Show Network, and NBC's *Celebrity Circus,* among others. Joey has also appeared on prank show *Impractical Jokers* and the inaugural season of the popular series *The Masked Singer.*

In his personal life, Joey was once linked to singer Pink (though it was apparently all rumors—the two were just friends) and eventually married his high school girlfriend Kelly Baldwin in 2004. Though the couple is now divorced, they share two daughters, Briahna (born in 2001) and Kloey (born in 2010), with Lance acting as godfather to both girls. Joey has been with current girlfriend Izabel Araujo for a number of years.

Whether or not NSYNC formally reunites and makes more music together, Joey seems content to keep working on the other side of entertainment, on small and big screens. As he told *Variety,* "[It's] completely different and people were seeing more of my personality as opposed to just being one of the guys from *NSYNC. And there's nothing wrong with being one of the guys from *NSYNC but people started to finally see that's Joey Fatone, he's a real personality, a host, an actor, a singer. So far, everything I've done no one has told me I sucked, which is great. As long as I don't have that, I think I'm good."

BROADWAY'S BOY BAND CONNECTION

Joey isn't the only famous boy band member to grace the Great White Way. A number of other veterans of the genre have been cast in various roles, from *Les Misérables* to *Wicked* and beyond, further showing off the ways in which they can sing, dance, and turn on the charm.

From pop stars to *Playbill*, here are some of the finest entertainment transplants.

Kevin Richardson: Beginning in 2003, the Backstreet Boy took a long break from the band to pursue his Broadway dreams when he was cast as lawyer Billy Flynn in the musical *Chicago*. It was a role he stayed with for years, including in international productions as far away as Japan.

Joey McIntyre: Before New Kids, Joey was just a kid working in local community theater. So when NKOTB took a break, he went back to his first love. Over the years, he's appeared in *tick, tick . . . BOOM!*, *Wicked*, *Waitress,* and even as The Fonz in an off-Broadway stage version of *Happy Days*.

Nick Jonas: The youngest member of the Jonas Brothers, Nick's first big break came on Broadway with pint-sized roles as a small child. His résumé includes parts in *Annie Get Your Gun, The Sound of Music, Beauty and the Beast,* and *A Christmas Carol*. He was even nominated for a Tony for his work in *Les Misérables*.

Drew Lachey: Drew may be best known as part of 98 Degrees with his brother, Nick, but his talents extend to various stage productions of *Rent* (like Joey, he also played the role of Mark), *Monty Python's Spamalot*, and *Hairspray* off-Broadway.

Ashley Parker Angel: The fellow Lou Pearlman protégé was a part of the *Making the Band* act O-Town, but also worked his magic in the theater in revivals of *Hairspray* and *Wicked*, remarking that, had the MTV series not popped up, he would have stayed the course with theater.

Chris Trousdale: The late talent was a member of Dream Street with Jesse McCartney in the late '90s and early 2000s. Before that, though, he was a Broadway star in productions of *Les Misérables* and *The Sound of Music*, among others.

LANCE EYES OUTER SPACE

> "I was certain from then on that my future was to be involved with space. It was the sky, not the stage, that first captured my creative imagination with such an extraordinary display of wonder."
>
> —Lance talking about a formative childhood trip to Cape Canaveral in his memoir, *Out of Sync*

What did Lance do during the NSYNC break? Well, he shot for the stars. A lot of kids say they want to be an astronaut when they grow up, but less than 1 percent get to do it. Unless you're Lance Bass, who actually had a shot to go into space in October 2002. After NSYNC's Celebrity Tour wrapped, Lance—just twenty-three at the time—moved to Russia to begin training as a cosmonaut in an attempt to become the youngest person ever in space.

All of it was part of a planned reality TV show, which would document the experience of a civilian (and celebrity) traveling to the International Space Station. But it came with a hefty price tag. Hollywood producers and agents intended to get sponsors (including what's been alluded to as a "popular breakfast drink") to pony up the estimated $20 million to confirm Lance's seat aboard the Soviet's Soyuz spacecraft.

As the story goes, in 2002 Lance and his personal manager were looking into new opportunities for the talent to take up during NSYNC's hiatus, to keep his name in the public eye, and that's when they got an offer that was truly out of this world. A TV executive got in touch, saying he had successfully bid on a seat for a future Soyuz flight for a civilian mission and he wanted Lance to fill it. The singer

Lance at the People's Choice Awards in 2002.

Lance listens to instructions during training at Johnson Space Center in Houston in August 2002.

actually thought he was being *Punk'd* when the offer came through.

As Lance shared in his *New York Times* best-selling 2007 memoir, *Out of Sync,* as picked up by *The Space Review,* "Very rarely do you get to have any of your big dreams actually come true. . . . I'd already had my pop-star fantasy realized with *NSYNC; now I was about to have a shot at the other, to be a spaceman."

And it was the all the handiwork of a nine-year-old fan, who was in the room when her parent and the TV producer were talking about their reality-TV outer-space pipe dream. Hearing the conversation, and remembering that Lance had talked about his dreams to be an astronaut in an AOL AMA session, the girl

suggested they consider the singer as their celebrity pick. A deal was soon struck, and Lance went through four months of intense training, including studying astrophysics and the Russian language, and even having a minor operation to repair a heart arrythmia to clear him for the mission.

"When I started training, NASA nor Roscosmos [Russia's official space department] believed in me at all. All they saw was, 'Oh, this boy band kid' . . . they all thought I was an alcoholic and a drug addict. Like they just thought 'rockstar, rockstar,'" Lance shared with the magazine *Futurism.* "They didn't think I would last a week."

The training (which Lance *did* effectively complete, making him a certified cosmonaut) was intense. As he told NPR, "It's not a tourist thing at all. I mean, you're a legit cosmonaut, and you're in charge of a lot of things. . . . I was in charge of all of our oxygen . . . so you know, I could at any moment kill everyone on board." Lance believed his training as part of the NSYNC machine only primed him for the mission. "It really did help me a lot. Just the discipline that we had to have to be in a group like that and the training that we had to go through to be able to perform like that and sing live. It kept me very grounded."

Sadly, the $20 million funding did not come in by the deadline and Lance was booted from the program, with his seat passing to another space crusader. The singer tried to salvage the opportunity, bringing in longtime supporter MTV and presenting a half-million of his own money to be able to go, but the efforts were futile. Several of the presenting sponsors had serious concerns about insurance clauses and the reputation they'd get if anything happened to Lance while he was out exploring the cosmos.

"What really hurt was that we had gone through so much and actually gotten so close. It was heartbreaking; there is no other word for it," Lance has said, noting that part of his drive was to get kids more interested in space and the sciences.

Instead, Lance took his experiences and passion and put it into becoming a youth spokesperson for World Space Week. He also sits on the board of governors for the National Space Society. And, in 2023, he launched a new podcast project, *The Last Soviet*, in which he shares the story of Sergei Krikalev, an astronaut who spent 311 days in outer space in 1991. "It's such an incredible story, obviously, one we didn't as Americans read in our history books, but it's interesting how things are still kind of following the same parallels even today," Lance told *Futurism*.

With his space invasion in the rearview, Lance moved on to other projects and pursuits. In the past two decades, he's helmed several production companies, including A Happy Place Productions, later known as Bacon & Eggs, and Lance Bass Productions. The firm also financed the 2014 documentary *Kidnapped for Christ*, about young teenagers in the Dominican Republic who were sent to "pray away the gay" programs.

Lance poses with his memoir at Barnes & Noble in New York in October 2007.

SHOWING HIS PRIDE

In the summer of 2006, four years into NSYNC's extended hiatus, Lance did an exclusive cover story with *People* magazine, revealing that he was gay. It was years ahead of New Kids On The Block boy bander Jonathan Knight doing the same in 2011, and came on the heels of gossip rags from *Page Six* to blogger Perez Hilton posting constant content and clickbait articles looking into Lance's sexuality.

Coming out in the *People* article (a last-minute grab that booted a planned Johnny Depp cover) was a huge deal for Lance, who said he often worried about how the news would impact not only his band but also his religious Southern Baptist family.

"I didn't know: Could that be the end of 'N Sync? So I had that weight on me of like, 'Wow, if I ever let anyone know, it's bad.' So I just never did," he told *People*. He hid behind a façade and became known as the "shy one" in the group, though it was just a defense mechanism to stay under the radar.

"I felt like if anyone found out that I was gay, the record label would immediately drop us and the fans would hate us—these were all the crazy things that went through my head as a teenager. So, I just trained myself into being a certain person and became that person," he clarified to *Huffington Post*. "Being onstage and singing those songs that you don't really relate to since you're talking about girls, it all, to me, wasn't real. Onstage, I just felt like I was playing a character the whole time."

Offstage, Lance tried to hide his sexuality, engaging in a high-profile relationship with actress Danielle Fishel (Topanga from *Boy Meets World,* pictured with Lance below) for a time. "So many people in the gay community go through having a girlfriend, and then realize, 'I'm gay—why am I with this girl?' And they realize how mean it is to put that girl through that," Lance remarked to the *Dallas Observer.* One of his first high-profile relationships after coming out was with Reichen Lehmkuhl, winner of Season 4 of *The Amazing Race.* Today, he's married to painter/actor/podcast co-host husband Michael Turchin, who he wed in 2014, and the couple are parents to twins, Alexander James and Violet Betty, born in 2021.

Lance's coming out was met with wide approval by fans and bandmates. In October 2006, Lance was honored with the Human Rights Campaign Visibility Award for the "positive, national conversation" that his reveal yielded.

That conversation is one that he continues to have, in particular with fans, as he shared during NSYNC's Hollywood Walk of Fame speech in 2018. "So many nights onstage, I'd see so many young, gay fans singing their hearts out and I wanted so badly to let you know, I was you," he said during the ceremony. "I just didn't have the strength then. But I do today and so let me say loud and proud to all my LGBT brothers and sisters, who embrace me and show me the way to be who I am, thank you so much."

his *Out of Sync* memoir was released, which further delved into his sexuality, and was a huge step for the boy bander who had remained closeted for years in an effort to not disrupt NSYNC's popularity. It was groundbreaking within the boy band world as well, as it would be another several years before New Kids' Jonathan Knight also came out. "I didn't want to offend anyone at that time," Lance told *USA Today* in 2024. "So I was so scared to speak out about it. But you know, I took the time to learn and to become a part of this community."

At the time Lance came out, gay marriage wasn't legal in the US and there was still a large stigma toward the LGBTQ+ community. He added to the paper, "Unfortunately, two decades ago, you did have to make those big, bold statements, and it was very, very scary—[it] changed my life. It changed my career for the good, for the bad. But it was also fun trying to navigate it and see where it took me, but it

In 2006, Lance came out in *People* magazine (see sidebar), with a huge cover story that declared, "I'm gay." It was shortly before

Lance and his dance partner, Lacey Schwimmer, rehearse for *Dancing with the Stars* in 2008.

made me grow as a human being and it made me become the person that I truly am. And I'm just so grateful for that."

Around that same time, Lance was also rumored to be working with the Logo network to put together an all-gay boy band. Nothing seems to have come of that venture, but in 2011, he was mentoring the male pop act Heart2Heart. Lance also formerly oversaw music management division Free Lance Entertainment, which had a partnership with Mercury Records to find new talent, particularly in the country realm, a style of music that Lance grew up loving. His family were also employed as talent scouts, though the enterprise eventually folded.

Like a number of his NSYNC colleagues, Lance also pursued acting projects, including minor roles on the WB show *7th Heaven* in 2000 and *Drop Dead Diva* in 2011, as well as in the movies *Zoolander* (2001), *Tropic Thunder* (2008), and *Cursed* (2011), in all the flicks, appearing as himself. He also did a brief stint on Broadway, in a reprisal of *Hairspray*. In 2015, he became a full-time contributor on the short-lived daytime talk program *The Meredith Vieira Show*. Lance also took an interest in a few reality opportunities, appearing on Season 7 of *Dancing with the Stars* (and coming in third place), as well as the FOX Network cooking competition show, *My Kitchen Rules,* in which he appeared with his mother, Diane (they were the runners up).

But it's radio and podcasts where Lance has really shone in recent years. In 2012, he had his own show, *Dirty Pop with Lance Bass*, on SiriusXM's OutQ station. And in 2023, he and now-husband Michael Turchin launched the very popular *Frosted Tips* podcast (a tongue-in-cheek reference to the go-to hairstyle of the 2000s), in which they interview '90s stars and, of course, boy band members. JC and NKOTB's Jonathan Knight were among the earliest guests, while Joey Fatone, Backstreet's AJ McLean and Howie Dorough, and New Kids' Donnie Wahlberg have also appeared.

"It started off that Nick Carter and I were going to do a show together (because we were both known for our frosted tips) . . . to give unsolicited life advice to the fans out there," Lance joked in an interview with MSN, though the show never panned out due to Nick's touring commitments with the Backstreet Boys. "So I pulled in my husband here and you know, we just go down memory lane with these amazing iconic boy band members because the fandoms for each group are huge and they're still so supportive and even Gen Z is jumping on board."

Lance has mentioned that he wants to expand the territory to cover all "teen idols," including a wish list that features *Saved By The Bell* star Mark-Paul Gosselaar and Jonathan Taylor Thomas. Over the podcast's several-dozen episodes to date, interview guests have included Sugar Ray's Mark McGrath, singer Debbie Gibson, Robbie Williams of Take That, Tiffany, and even NSYNC manager Johnny Wright.

Lance also told *Billboard* of the *Frosted Tips* podcast that he wanted it to be a safe space to "tell stories we were never allowed to tell before," adding, "We had to keep it very PG back in the day. And there was a lot of stuff going down behind the curtain. There's definitely a lot of secrets being told. It's a really great look at the music industry, especially in that era. . . . A lot of the issues we were dealing with at the time were kept out of public view because we didn't want the fans to know."

Lance and then-fiancé (now husband) Michael Turchin at the SiriusXM studios in 2013, broadcasting *Dirty Pop with Lance Bass*.

CHRIS FINDS HIS OTHER VOICE

"After 'N Sync, I had this phobia about going back in front of the public. Especially after the success of Justin and JC. I felt a lot of personal pressure on me. But, in the end, I told myself I'm not Justin and JC. I can't try to hold myself to such a high standard. I have to go with it and enjoy."

—Chris talking to the *Orlando Sentinel* in 2007

The man who started it all in 1995 is also the one who has probably changed the most over the last two decades. During NSYNC's hiatus, Chris has tried out a variety of different endeavors and spread his wings into surprising new territory, from clothing to country music to hosting events for Arnold Schwarzenegger.

In the early 2000s, Chris spent the boy band break attached to another label: a fashion label. Even before the split, Chris was developing his clothing line, FuMan Skeeto, and he had the chance to debut it at New York Fashion Week 2001. Described as "urban-inspired women's streetwear with an Asian influence," fans of all ages and genders could buy T-shirts, tank tops, skirts, jeans, and

Chris at the annual MAGIC International Fashion Convention in 2002, promoting his clothing line, FuMan Skeeto.

sweatsuits cut up with leather, rhinestones, and denim (the total look of the 2000s) at retailers like Nordstrom and Bloomingdale's.

The idea for the brand was birthed when the singer saw a number of NSYNC fans wearing a ton of FUBU-branded wear and sports apparel, and he figured he could enter the arena, especially as other music acts like J. Lo and P. Diddy did so (the latter with his line Sean John). Chris spoke to *Women's Wear Daily* in the spring of 2001, saying he came up with the name of his line while spending a night writing music in a hotel room with friends, during which he had a curious run-in with a mosquito. "My initials are CK, and I couldn't use that since some guy already has it," he jokingly added to *WWD*.

But FuMan Skeeto didn't stick around for long, and other than working as a voiceover actor playing the character of Chip Skylark from 2001–2009 on the long-running Nickelodeon show, *The Fairly OddParents*, Chris took a bit of a break from the limelight when NSYNC parted. He even turned down the chance to play Jesus in a Broadway revival of *Jesus Christ Superstar* around 2003. It was a time when he was partying hard and in a self-described "funk."

Then VH1 came calling, with the proposal for a show called *Mission: Man Band*. It debuted in 2007, with an aim to bring together former bright stars in boy bands to try to make the magic happen again with a new, more mature pop act. Chris provided his Orlando home to serve as the show's commune and invited his fellow *Man Band* cohorts—LFO's Rich Cronin, 98 Degrees' Jeff Timmons, and Color Me Badd's Bryan Abrams—to move in and work together with an all-star team of songwriters,

producers, vocal coaches, and talent managers.

And even though nothing really came of the show (and the guys were even booed while performing at an Orlando Magic game), "It made me work," Chris told the *Orlando Sentinel*. "It made me stop hiding in my studio like a hermit. . . . I gained a lot of weight. I was doing this excessive partying. I had to do something about my bad habits."

He further explained those bad habits to *Huffington Post*, clarifying that they came early on during the NSYNC hiatus: "I made the mistake of being too complacent and realizing that, man, I got this celebrity-ism and all these things going for me, so I'm going to spend the next few years of my life just partying my ass off. I was young enough where I thought that was the right thing to do. And looking back, I had so many opportunities and there was so much I could have done."

Once he got back in the groove, though, Chris made up for lost time, throwing himself into a number of projects, including trying his hand at new music. *Super* new. The projects he wound up in took huge leaps from NSYNC, as he found himself dabbling in country and alt rock. In 2008, Chris was a contestant on the second season of the CMT reality show *Gone Country*, in which a handful of celebrities uproot to Nashville, work with in-demand songwriters and producers, and compete for the chance at a country music career, with the winner getting a single produced by John Rich of Big & Rich. In his season, Chris was up against fellow contestants Jermaine Jackson of the Jackson 5, *Fame* star Irene Cara, and hair metal icon Sebastian Bach, who ended up winning.

Chris with (L to R) Jeff Timmons, Rich Cronin, and Bryan Abrams, stars of VH1's *Mission: Man Band*, in 2007.

WHAT'S IN A NAME?

Chris has hit a lot of milestones in his 50-plus years of life—not the least of which was birthing NSYNC. But was the moment he really made it when he was included on a diss track by Eminem? To some people, maybe. The rapper (pictured here) name-drops Chris and says he can get his "ass kicked" in the 2002 track "Without Me" from *The Eminem Show* album, including Chris in a short rant against other artists of the day like Limp Bizkit and Moby. But why?

In May of that year, Eminem went on MTV's *TRL* to explain, telling the network it was because, "Kirkpatrick was the only boy band member who had the guts to say something" back to him, with the network adding, it was "after the rapper attacked the group and boy bands in general on his last album."

Chris responded to the escapade, albeit about 20 years later, in an appearance on the *Insight with Chris Van Vliet* in 2021, saying, "At first, I was kind of freaked out and of course, nowadays it's amazing because that song is one of my favorite songs and then to have my name at the end in it too, it's just like, I did something right. Or wrong."

Chris said he believed it stemmed from a time NSYNC was on *TRL* and he casually mentioned that Eminem "was like the crocodile hunter with controversy. . . . In my mind I was thinking he's got good music but he probably took it as I was saying that the only reason he's popular is because he's controversial."

The singer remembers the day the song first came out, telling the interviewer, "I was getting all of these text messages and everyone was like, 'Yo have you heard the new Eminem song? He makes fun of you in it.' And I was like, 'Yeah he always does, NSYNC rhymes with everything.' They're like, 'No, you!' I'm like, 'What do you mean me? He says Chris Kirkpatrick? What the hell rhymes with Chris Kirkpatrick?' Then, I heard 'get your ass kicked' and I said, 'Oh, yeah. That does rhyme.'"

Chris with host John Rich (center) and actor Lorenzo Lamas (left) of *Gone Country* in 2008.

"I just wanted to learn what it was like, how it's written, because it's a completely different style of music than what I'm used to with rock, pop, and R&B," Chris told *OK Magazine* in 2008. "Everything about the writing style and the music is different in this genre. . . . I love being around music, no matter whether I'm behind the console or in front of the crowd."

At the time of the show's airing, Chris had gotten so immersed in the country scene, he was eyeing a move to Nashville (which he eventually did in 2016), and started his own production company, Working Class Industries, to bring in some of the genre's elite, like Kenny Chesney.

Around the same time, he also started a new music group called Nigel's 11. It was an alternative rock act where Chris finally took his turn on lead vocals and was joined by Orlando friends Mike Bosch on guitar, Dave Carreiro on

bass, and Ernie Longoria on drums. "I felt very much a part of *NSync. Everybody had a role— Justin and JC had the leads, and I did a lot of background because I have that voice," Chris told journalist Heather Laude about getting his chance as a frontman. "Now it's much different. It's a completely new thing for me to work toward and have to learn."

The band, who claimed to be influenced by classic arena rock acts like Queen, Boston, and ELO, first formed in 2007 and started working on their debut album in 2009. Though they were unsigned by a major label, they were managed by NSYNC's Johnny Wright. Their one and only album, *Clandestine Operation*, was self-released in 2010.

Eventually, Chris found his footing writing music for others, like David Foster, AJ McLean, and Tony Lucca, and, curiously enough, was appearing in a number of music videos from artists like Fall Out Boy,

The Hummingbird (aka Chris) in *The Masked Singer* in 2022.

Good Charlotte, and A Day To Remember. According to *Alternative Press*, he loved the pop punk scene and wanted to have at least a small part in it.

Like the rest of NSYNC, Chris had his moment to shine in a few other featured spots in TV shows and movies. In the reality TV realm, he competed on Season 3 of *Celebrity Big Brother* in 2022 and was on *The Masked Singer* as the "Hummingbird" that same year. Chris also joined Joey Fatone in Joey McIntyre's series, *Return of the Mac*, and Nick Carter's zombie horror film, *Dead 7.* Chris had bit roles in TV series *Angie Tribeca* in 2016 and the TV movie *Sharknado 3* in 2015. Oh, and then there are the talent and teen pageants he hosts for Arnold Schwarzenegger as part of his Arnold Sports Festival in Columbus, Ohio, every year.

With his hands tied in so many projects, Chris still found time to develop his personal life, marrying Karlyn M. Skladany in 2013. The couple welcomed son Nash Dylan in 2017. At the moment, Chris seems to enjoy the responsibilities that come with being a father and remaining, for the most part, behind the scenes. "I've got a three-and-a-half-year-old kid that keeps me busy eight days a week, which is awesome," he told *Variety* in 2021.

But when it comes to the possibility of making his own solo music, Chris told *Page Six* in late 2022, "I think my time has passed," though hinting to "never say never" to the idea of NSYNC coming around again. "We had a run in the band, and if the band goes back out again, sure, you know, we'll all sit down and talk about things that way."

In Sync with NSYNC

My name is Casey and I have NSYNC Fan Problems. It's nothing new; this has been the case for twenty-something years of my life. The *No Strings Attached* tapestry adorns my kitchen wall. The only item on my bucket list is to have all five members sign my custom-made NSYNC sneakers (I'm currently at three). I once ran on a treadmill next to Chris Kirkpatrick while wearing a shirt with his name on it. I was a regular at Justin Timberlake's Manhattan location of Southern Hospitality . . . and I live in Massachusetts. On vacations as a teenager, I would beg my parents to take me to a Virgin Megastore so I could search for the European version of the debut album. (We found it in Miami and it's still one of my most prized possessions.)

But my story isn't necessarily unique. When I started @nsyncfanprobs in 2013, I quickly realized there were many more like me: people who had fallen in love with this boy band early on and continued to support the guys through the hiatus (because, yes, it is a hiatus). Why? I don't know exactly, but it's some combination of superior harmonies, iconic choreography, and a brotherhood that has endured. I've made incredible friends, had once-in-a-lifetime experiences (see the treadmill comment above), and danced and sang my heart out to their music more times than I could count. I'm so grateful for the five of them. And I'll happily have NSYNC Fan Problems for the rest of my life.

Casey Lennon

THE BIG TEASE

"It's funny, because when we were all together, everything jumped back. I felt 10 years younger. There wasn't any real bickering and nobody had any animosity, which we have had before when there were little problems amongst us. But it's all water under the bridge. We just enjoyed being around each other. I can't count anything in, but I can't count anything out either."

—Chris talking to *Rolling Stone* after the band appeared together at the 2013 VMAs

If you count up all the headlines over the years, there have probably been about as many speculating on an NSYNC reunion as there have been NSYNC albums sold. Much of it was just hopelessly devoted fans reading into *everything* as a possible clue that the band was rethinking things. All five were in attendance for Chris's wedding in 2013—this is the sign! They were together for JC's fortieth birthday in 2016—it must be happening! But the band *has* auspiciously set some things in motion—including their latest quasi-reunion at the 2023 VMAs—that have kept an iron-clad fanbase waiting on bated breath ever since.

In 2003, there was that Bee Gees tribute at the 45th annual Grammys; in 2004, they sang the national anthem together at the NSYNC Challenge for the Children; in 2005, there was the *Greatest Hits* compilation (followed by 2010's *The Collection* and 2014's *The Essential *NSYNC*). But there was nothing that presented more solid evidence, to many, than their 2013 regrouping at that year's VMAs to help honor Justin as he received the Michael Jackson Video Vanguard Award.

Lance, JC, Justin, Joey, and Chris reunite at the 2013 MTV Video Music Awards.

NSYNC performs at
the 2003 Grammys.

Weeks ahead of the performance in August 2013, Justin called up the guys to ask for a favor. Chris later recalled the conversation to *Rolling Stone*, remembering that Justin said, "'I'm getting this award, and I'm wondering if you think the other guys might be interested in coming and performing?' I was like, 'For you, of course.'"

Whatever hurt feelings and confusion had surrounded the band after Justin broke the news to them in 2004 that he was done with NSYNC has seemingly cleared up over the years, with the comradery of the five former bandmates allowing for events like the 2013 VMAs reunion to happen. As *Huffington Post* explained in their interview with JC, Joey, Chris, and Lance in 2018, "Overall, the four members of *NSYNC who aren't Justin Timberlake had nothing but nice things to say about him, calling him their super-talented 'little brother.'" Never once did they contemplate moving ahead without him either. As Chris told *Rolling Stone*, "We've never kicked that idea around. The band is who the band is. . . . . We're not 'NSync without all five of us."

So, when Justin called upon his former cohorts to help fete the night at the 2013 VMAs, there was no hesitation. But there was work to do. It had been ten years since the band last performed together and they only had a two-week heads-up to get things sorted for the medley of "Girlfriend" and "Bye Bye Bye" (which ended up being only about 90 seconds long, but still). The rest of the boy band flew to Miami, where Justin had just wrapped a leg of his solo tour, and started working, holding rehearsals in convention rooms at the Fillmore Hotel.

"[My choreography] definitely didn't come back quickly. I was the one that was cursing a lot and fumbling around," Chris joked to *Rolling Stone*, admitting that he and Lance were the worst during those rehearsals (true to how it had been during the band's heyday, he added).

The hardest part, though, was not re-learning the dance moves, but keeping everything a secret. "It got leaked a bit, so that's when people started going, 'I've been hearing rumors. What's going on?'" Chris remembered. Their cars were followed going to rehearsals and paparazzi caught members having drinks together. "People were putting it up [online] all over the place," he added. "Back in the day, we never really had any social media. We had a website. That was pretty much all the social media we had, so now it's almost like a whole new world for us," he said. "I think my followers doubled just in the week we were in Miami and New York."

Once they got inside the Barclays Arena in Brooklyn, where the VMAs were being held, another secret operation began. As Lance recalled to CBS, "We had to perform in the middle of the arena, so there was no way of getting us out there without being seen. So they dressed us in big ole hoodies to pretend we were the stagehands. . . . We would push out the stage and do all the stagehand stuff until we got to the area and hid out beneath a staircase."

Chris described the night as "magical" and said that "just the fact that we got that moment together again—we enjoyed every second of it."

The rest of the world agreed. In fact, as *Business Insider* reported shortly after the performance aired, "everyone went insane when 'NSYNC reunited at the VMAs." The outlet turned to that trusty Twitterverse, which had by then become a part of the boy band empire, to grab some of the best fan comments from the night.

"Nobody cared when Backstreet reunited but a whole generation of 30-somethings died during the #nsync reunion," said one person. "It's ok to cry right now," said another. Even *People* magazine had thoughts: "How are we all doing? Are we okay? Did all the rhinestones fall out of our collective bandanas at once?" But it was Target's corporate Twitter that had the real zinger: "That high-pitched squealing? Yeah, that was us. Screaming like 12-year-old girls."

Of course, nothing followed the event (and it would be another 10 years until the band teased fans again at the 2023 VMAS—are we sensing a theme?). Right after the 2013 performance, Lance confirmed to CBS that "we've got nothing planned."

It would be another five years before another big moment brought the five guys back together, but it was worth the wait. On April 30, 2018, NSYNC received the 2,636th star on the famous Hollywood Walk of Fame, in a spot that may as well be known as boy band central (their star is near those of Backstreet Boys, Boyz II Men, New Kids On The Block, and New Edition).

ABOVE: Chris, Lance, JC, Joey, and Justin gather in Hollywood to celebrate their star on the Walk of Fame in 2018.

INSET: NSYNC's star on the Walk of Fame.

USA Today called it an "emotional reunion," which included induction speeches from pals like Carson Daly (who helped introduce the band to the world on *TRL* those many moons ago) and Ellen DeGeneres, who had the band on her talk show several times, including the same day they received their star.

Carson jokingly started his speech, "When I was first approached about speaking at the Hollywood Walk of Fame ceremony to honor one of the biggest groups in *TRL* history, I thought to myself, 'Oh god, they're giving Limp Bizkit a star!'" He went on to heartfully add, "I'm honored to be here to tell you a little bit about one of the most successful groups to ever walk through our doors at MTV. . . . perhaps my greatest achievement occurred

back in 1998, when a boy band came to the US, hot off the charts in Europe, and landed on our MTV doorsteps in Times Square. . . . I got to be a part of history as America met and

NSYNC HEADS TO COACHELLA

When Ariana Grande headlined Coachella in 2019, she had something special planned to mark the occasion: a performance from NSYNC. Well, four-fifths of the band anyway (Justin was enmeshed in his Man of the Woods Tour at the time).

JC, Joey, Lance, and Chris joined the pop star for weekend one of the desert event, coming out near the start of her performance to help Ariana with her track, "break up with your girlfriend, i'm bored." The five of them then whipped out a grandiose cover of NSYNC's "Tearin' Up My Heart" that put people into a tailspin. The moment all but broke the internet when fans found out. "*NSYNC PERFORMING WITH ARIANA AT COACHELLA IS EVERYTHING I NEVER KNEW I NEEDED!" said one fan (in all caps, for emphasis).

In fact, the performance was so well received it led *Rolling Stone* to assert that it was proof NSYNC should consider touring without Justin, saying the appearance "proves they don't need their biggest star to reunite." Afterwards Joey tweeted, "Thanks @arianagrande for having us . . . was a great time and a chance to perform with my brothers once again."

Astute viewers of NSYNC's 1999 pay-per-view special probably saw this coming. In footage of "Thinking of You (I Drive Myself Crazy)," filmed at a Ft. Lauderdale concert that year, the camera pans over to a young fan in the crowd, watching it all in her mother's arms. That child just so happened to be Ariana Grande.

"We were not only enjoying it and hoping that our fans would enjoy it and doing it for them, but then now our fans are becoming these people as well," Chris told *People* magazine of the transition of the band's fans into megastars in their own right.

Fans celebrate the band's Walk of Fame star on April 30, 2018.

fell in love with NSYNC for the very first time on US television."

When it came time for the guys' speeches, JC began, thanking their longtime vocal coach Robin Wiley for her contributions, hailing her as the "apostrophe or star" in the band's name and then turning to his bandmates and thanking them for "making my dreams come true."

Chris turned to the guys' families, expressing his gratitude to them all for being part of the journey and telling his young son, Nash, "You have some of the best uncles on the planet."

Lance said he wanted to "say something I've been trying to put into words maybe my whole life," explaining that, "growing up in

Mississippi in a Southern Baptist church in a town where everyone knows your business, I had a secret. I was gay." He said he was proud to be able to proudly proclaim himself part of the LGBTQ+ community and thanked LGBTQ+ fans for their support.

Joey also turned his attention to the fans in his speech, saying, "It's amazing that we've never had an album in years, and you guys are still supporting us to this day."

Last up was Justin, who remarked, "These four guys mean so much to me and we're really a family and the memories that we have and the times that we've shared and the families that we've built from it, I don't think I can really put into words how much the four of you mean to me. Through hard times, through unbelievable times . . . I just love all you so much." His words clearly moved the other four, who moved in for a group hug.

And, of course, what kind of NSYNC event would it be without one more reunion tease? Justin just had to get hopes up for all the fans in attendance and those watching the livestream at home by ending his speech with, "We've had an incredible ride and I can't wait to see what the future holds."

As *Billboard* reported, once the guys exited the red carpet area, the huge flock of fans in the crowd started "a chant of 'RE-U-NITE!' that continued for a minute" and did a crowd sing-along of "Tearin' Up My Heart," perhaps symbolizing what the years of NSYNC's absence has meant.

There's still hope. "Never say never," Lance told *Billboard* in 2023, just months before the other big VMAs moment. "I think it just has to be the right time; we all have to be inspired in the moment. But I do think the world needs something again from *NSYNC. I always feel bad that there was no ending, because we didn't have a final show, we didn't have a final tour, because we didn't know it was the final days. I think we owe it to the fans to give them something at some point. I just hope it's before I'm 80 years old."

The guys backstage at the 2013 MTV Video Music Awards.

PART III
I WANT YOU BACK

A reunion ten years in the
making: NSYNC at the
2023 MTV Video Music Awards.

IN A "BETTER PLACE"

> "I had your dolls. Like, are you doing something? What's going to happen now? They're going to do something and I need to know what it is."
>
> —Taylor Swift, after receiving an award from NSYNC at the 2023 VMAs

And just like that, they were back! On September 12, 2023, NSYNC once again shocked the MTV VMAs audience—and the world, for that matter—with a surprise, unannounced appearance on the telecast, as all five guys presented the Best Pop Award. The winner: a very shocked, very fangirling Taylor Swift. Upon seeing Justin, JC, Joey, Chris, and Lance come onto the stage, Taylor jumped up from her seat, hands over her mouth in total shock, like any other regular fan doing the same at home in front of their TVs.

"Over 20 years ago, we were just kids when we won best pop video for 'Bye Bye Bye,'" JC began, competing with the deafening roar of the audience. "It was our first VMA and it meant the world to us." Chris then took over, sharing, "That award validated our hard work," while Joey thanked MTV and "each and every one of the fans" for sticking by the band.

Joey, Lance, Justin, JC, and Chris onstage at the 2023 MTV Video Music Awards.

195

Taylor Swift accepts her 2023 Best Pop MTV Video Music Award as NSYNC looks on.

After Taylor was handed her Moon Man award (and some friendship bracelets from Lance), she was speechless, eventually managing, "I'm not doing well pivoting from this to this" as she gestured from NSYNC back to her award. Rather than start with her own speech, she spoke aloud the question on everyone's mind: "Are you doing something? What's going to happen now?"

This time around, more than any other "soft" reunion, it has really felt like NSYNC was up to something. Just weeks prior to the VMAs appearance, rumors bounced across the internet and social media that NSYNC was getting the band back together, after a trailer

dropped for the new animated movie, *Trolls Band Together*.

Justin has long been part of the franchise and accompanying soundtracks. In this third iteration of the film, his character, Branch, took on a unique storyline in which he took part in a boy band reunion with his long-lost brothers. It hit a little too close to home, leaving fans to wonder if they should read between the lines. At the time of the trailer release, *Entertainment Tonight* reported that JC, Joey, Chris, and Lance "are expected to have surprise roles" in the film, according to a reliable source close to the band.

Sure enough, two days after the VMAs surprise, NSYNC confirmed the rumors, announcing that not only were they to be part of *Trolls Band Together* but they also planned to release a new song for its soundtrack, called "Better Place"—their first new song in more than 20 years.

"It was pretty emotional, the first time we all got in the studio together. Back in March [2023], we decided to, you know, get back together and have some fun and it was like no [time] had passed," Lance said to *Entertainment Tonight* of recording with his boy band brothers again. "It is beautiful, you know? To be this age and the fans are still this excited, it is a dream come true. I had no idea the fandom would go this nuts."

Less than two weeks after the official release of "Better Place" on September 29, the track shot up the *Billboard Hot 100*, movement that NSYNC hasn't seen since 2002. It peaked at No. 25 and spent six full weeks on the chart.

Not too shabby for an elder boy band who, as of now, have only announced the one single.

But could more be coming? After all, NSYNC does have an all-important thirtieth anniversary coming in 2025, making the time ripe for a fully-fledged reunion (for real, this time). And, with the reaction at the VMAs (which Lance has gone as far to say was a result of the powerful Taylor Swift Swifties machine), there's clearly a market for it.

Not to mention, the guys have all but been hinting at it. In December 2023, Lance made an appearance on a game show called *Rent Free* in which the host asked if a reunion was imminent. Lance responded, "We are talking about it—and I hope to have some good news, at some point."

Joey has also chimed in on the topic, telling *People* magazine in December 2023,

The band backstage at the 2023 MTV Video Music Awards.

A MOMENT OF
TOTAL "PARADISE"

And then it happened. After 11 long years, NSYNC finally reunited on stage to perform music together once again—and not just four of the five guys. Justin was there too. In fact, it happened during a night meant to celebrate Justin's sixth solo album, *Everything I Thought It Was*.

Two days ahead of JT's latest solo album drop, the singer held an intimate show at Los Angeles's Wiltern Theatre on March 13, 2024, just miles from where NSYNC's star lives on the Hollywood Walk of Fame. (Chris, Lance, and Justin are pictured below, at the official release party the following night.) The night was part of a series of small one-night-only shows Justin had been staging in cities like New York and Memphis in 2024 to help promote the new album and act as a warmup to his sold-out world tour.

But, when it came time to wrap up the LA gig, he had the surprise of all surprises for the small crowd gathered inside the venue. Joey, JC, Chris, and Lance joined him for a four-song set that included early NSYNC hits "Girlfriend," "Bye Bye Bye," and "It's Gonna Be Me," as well as JT's new solo song "Paradise," a track that features his four boy band brothers as special guests.

The Wiltern set was the group's first time performing as a unit again since coming together to fete JT's Video Vanguard Award honor at the VMAs in 2013. And it was yet another strong tease of a possible fully-fledged NSYNC reunion with rumors flying since the guys worked on a song for the *Trolls* soundtrack in 2023.

As *Variety* reported in their recap of the Wiltern surprise set, "Fans in the audience were deeply moved; tears were streaming down faces." The article added that, as the five guys took their seats on a row of stools to sing the tender ballad, "Paradise . . . Harmonies flew, eyes were wet, and they stood at the front of the stage at the end, soaking up the rapturous applause."

Could this be the sign of more to come? Possibly. After JT posted a photo of the five empty stools on Instagram, Lance was quick to comment, "That was fun. Let's do it again soon."

"You know what? Never say never. I think we have to honestly have a sit-down and have a conversation." He also clarified his thoughts, adding, "There's been talks about, 'Do we want to do something?' and 'How are we gonna do it?' But nothing's in motion yet. . . . I'm not saying no, and I'm not saying yes. But we still have to have that conversation. It looks promising."

At pre-Grammys festivities in February 2024, JC also talked to *Billboard* on the red carpet and teased, "We might have another one after 'Better Place,' we might have been cooking a little bit," adding, "There is that element, I know it sounds cliché, but it's as if we never left."

All five guys also appeared on the popular interview series *Hot Ones*, in which subjects eat increasingly spicy chicken wings as they answer increasingly salacious questions.

In addition to the veiled comments about a possible reunion, one of the biggest revelations was when Justin told the host that he "did in fact get a 'note' from a producer to pronounce 'me' like 'may' in 'It's Gonna Be Me.'"

But perhaps one of the most shocking admissions came from Justin himself. In an appearance on *The Kelly Clarkson Show* in late January 2024, Justin spilled some details, sharing, "We've been in the studio, so there may be a little something in the future too." He added that working with his four boy bandmates again felt right: "It's kind of crazy, like, there's so much that just picks up right where it left off as far as the chemistry."

Even more curious was the timing. Justin announced his sixth studio album, *Everything I Thought It Was*, and dropped the first single, "Selfish," in late January 2024, with a cycle of

The guys arrive together at the *Trolls Band Together* premiere in Hollywood on November 15, 2023.

Justin on *The Kelly Clarkson Show* in 2024.

promotion including heading to *Saturday Night Live* as a repeat musical guest. He spoke to Apple Music's Zane Lowe about the new effort, claiming he wrote 100 songs and narrowed it down to 18 for the new album. On *The Kelly Clarkson Show,* Justin has said his solo career has turned him into a "studio rat," which gives him ample time to write and record. On the heels of the news, Justin also announced a new solo tour, the Forget Tomorrow World Tour, that took him around the globe through most of 2024.

Not that the other guys have stayed dormant while they decide the future of NSYNC. In early 2024, Chris announced he was taking part in and hosting the return of the Pop 2000 Tour, which includes a lineup of O-Town, BBMAK, Ryan Cabrera, and LFO across 26 dates in North America. And Joey and Backstreet Boys' AJ McLean announced a new string of dates together called

A Legendary Night Tour, which hit a number of clubs across America in March 2024. JC also worked with One Direction's Liam Payne on a new collaboration song, telling *Billboard*, "Working with him was an absolute joy."

Whether or not a full NSYNC reunion comes to fruition, there's no doubt the memories, the excitement, the music domination, and the fans have remained on the minds and hearts of all five members over the years—and will continue to do so forever. As Chris told *People* magazine, "My wife likes to play scratch-off lottery tickets and all that. And I'm always like, I don't need to play the lottery. I already won the lottery. . . . few people have ever lived [or] have gotten to have this experience and do what I've done. And to have that, to have that going forward . . . I could lose everything and still have everything—[to] still have those memories and those moments and that time."

In Sync with NSYNC

My name is Ana Caraig and I've been an NSYNC fan ever since their *Disney: In Concert* aired on the Disney Channel in 1998. My cousin was a huge *Mickey Mouse Club* fan and told me to watch it because two guys from the show were now in this boyband NSYNC. So we watched it together and the energy alone in the opening number—heck, even when they're walking onto the stage—was so crazy that I couldn't help but keep my eyes glued to the TV. I fell hard for the guys that day and continue to support them in any way possible. I've attended numerous concerts (as a group, their solo shows, and collab shows), TV appearances, Vegas appearances, etc.

One of the most epic moments for me was attending a *Price Is Right* show in Las Vegas that Joey was hosting. It was for my twenty-eighth birthday and I was decked out in a shirt that I thought for sure would get a producer's attention or get me on stage. It said, "I love Joey Fatone" up front and on the back it read, "Pick me and I'll even bust out my NSYNC dance moves." So when the second round of names got called, I lost my mind when I heard mine. I ran out of the aisle so fast, not caring who I was stepping on, and when I got on stage, I immediately hugged Joey and happy-cried my eyes out. When it was my turn to get interviewed, he immediately said, "Okay, let's see those dance moves," and I was ready but then asked, "No music?" In my head, I'm thinking a DJ would play some track they had ready in case of fans like myself. But to my surprise, Joey himself started singing "Tearin' Up My Heart," and I busted out the routine beside him. I didn't care that I didn't win anything during the game because the moment made me feel like I won the jackpot.

Since their dreadful "hiatus," the most memorable moment for me has to be attending their Hollywood pop-up shop as well as their Hollywood Walk of Fame ceremony. I attended all four days of the pop-up hoping for surprise appearances and bought every single piece of merch that day. Hence my NSYNC memorabilia account on Instagram: @nsync.freak. But the energy of the crowd at the Walk of Fame ceremony was so insane, and all of us just singing our hearts out to the guys; it's definitely something I will never forget.

Being a fan since 1998, I am stuck on a goal I've been trying to achieve since my love began for this group. I hope to one day accomplish getting all five guys to sign my copy of their debut album. I've got three down and two more to go (possibly the two hardest ones) and hope to accomplish that one day in the future.

Ana Caraig

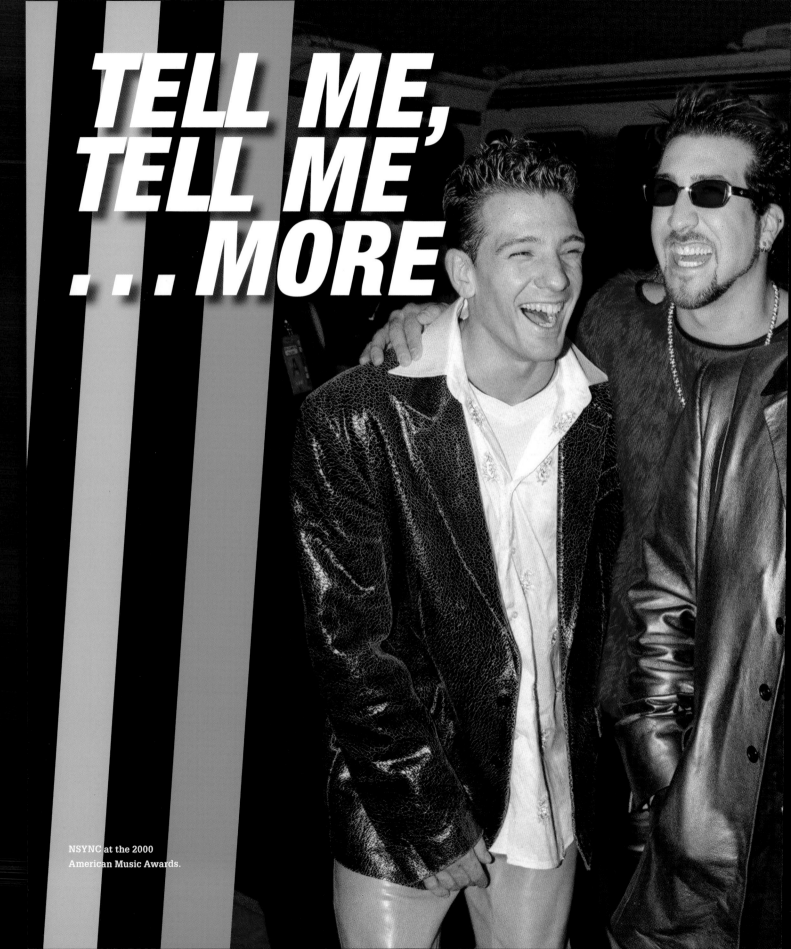

TELL ME, TELL ME' ...MORE

NSYNC at the 2000
American Music Awards.

TIMELINE

1994

While working at Universal Studios as part of the doo-wop groupe the Hollywood Hi-Tones, Chris Kirkpatrick decides he wants to form his own band. Through college friend (and Backstreet Boy) Howie Dorough, he hears BSB's manager Lou Pearlman is looking to start up a new act. After a meeting, Lou tells Chris that if he can find four other guys to be in the boy band, he'll fund the group.

1995

NSYNC is officially formed in Orlando.

October 1995: NSYNC plays their first seminal gig at Disney World's Pleasure Island in Orlando to thousands of fans, thanks to the ingenuity of Justin's mom, Lynn.

1996

After NSYNC has issues trying to get approval from American record executives, they get their first contract in Europe with BMG Ariola Munich. The band moves to the continent and starts working with Swedish producers Denniz Pop and Max Martin, who were the ones to write "I Want You Back" and "Tearin' Up My Heart."

October 7, 1996: NSYNC puts out their first single, "I Want You Back," in Europe; by mid-November, it lands a Top 10 spot on the German music charts.

1997

February 10, 1997: "Tearin' Up My Heart" is released as the second single in Germany and European territories; it also claims a Top 10 spot on the charts.

May 5, 1997: "Here We Go" is the third single NSYNC releases overseas, climbing up to the No. 6 spot.

May 26, 1997: NSYNC's self-titled debut is released in Europe; by its second week on the streets, it hits the No. 1 spot on the German charts; 800,000 copies of the album are sold in Eastern Europe.

August 18, 1997: A fourth single, "For The Girl Who Has Everything," is released as the band's star grows. The success leads to the band embarking on the For The Girl Tour around Europe that summer.

November 3, 1997: A final debut album single, "Together Again," is released as the band continues to tour; it's also the month that BMG's American rep Vince DeGiorgio happens to be in attendance at NSYNC's show in Budapest and works to sign them to the US market. A few short weeks later, they have a record deal that brings them home to America.

1998

January 20, 1998: NSYNC's first single in the US, "I Want You Back," is released; it's also their first American music video.

March 24, 1998: NSYNC's self-titled debut album is released in the US, though it has some changes from the European original. Unfortunately, *NSYNC* has a dismal debut, entering the *Billboard* Top 200 chart at No. 82.

June 11, 1998: The band's first US tour, NSYNC In Concert, kicks off and travels to smaller clubs. It runs through September 23 and is later rebranded as the Second II None Tour in November, playing larger arenas.

June 30, 1998: As it was in Europe, "Tearin' Up My Heart" is the second single released in America, alongside a music video. Both that song and "I Want You Back" start being serviced to radio, which helps bring both tracks to the *Billboard Hot 100* charts.

July 18, 1998: A pivotal moment comes for NSYNC when they're tapped for the *Disney: In Concert* special after the Backstreet Boys pull out of the gig. After it's televised on July 18, it turns the band into overnight sensations.

October 1998: NSYNC's debut album shoots to the No. 2 spot on the *Billboard 200* chart and stays there for 109 weeks total, including 30 weeks spent within the Top 10.

October 14, 1998: NSYNC is added on to a leg of Janet Jackson's Velvet Rope Tour for two weeks. It's some of NSYNC's first major public appearances, bringing them to mainstream audiences.

November 10, 1998: The band's one and only holiday album, *Home For Christmas*, is released. The band also nabs their first *Rolling Stone* feature this month.

1999

Britney and Justin start dating after the former Mouseketeers are linked up again on NSYNC's Second II None Tour, in which Britney opens several January and February dates.

February 9, 1999: "(God Must Have Spent) A Little More Time on You" is released as the third US single and hits No. 8 on the *Billboard Hot 100* chart; a week later in February, "Thinking of You (I Drive Myself Crazy)" is released as the final single from the debut album.

March 1999: NSYNC's initial tour is rebranded again as the Ain't No Stoppin' Us Now Tour (running through June) and then again as the Boys of Summer Tour (kicking off in July and running through September). By the time it's done, it's the third-highest-grossing tour of 1999.

November 1999: The members of NSYNC come to the realization that Lou Pearlman is scamming them out of their rightful earnings and attempt to leave their contract with Trans Continental Records. Lou and BMG slap the five with a breach of contract lawsuit worth $150 million; the court case begins in November but is quickly settled out of court in December as NSYNC signs with a new label, Jive Records.

2000

January 17, 2000: NSYNC releases new music from their upcoming album, the first single being "Bye Bye Bye," a statement about bidding adieu to Pearlman.

March 11, 2000: NSYNC appears on *Saturday Night Live* for the first and only time, in an episode hosted by *Dawson's Creek* star Joshua Jackson.

March 21, 2000: The much-anticipated *No Strings Attached* is released. The album sells 2.41 million copies in its first week, including 1.1 million on release day alone, and sets a new record for first-week sales.

May 9, 2000: The 50-plus-date No Strings Attached Tour begins; it's a completely sold-out affair, which wraps up December 1. NSYNC sells the most tickets of any tour in 2000, bringing in $76.4 million.

May 16, 2000: *No Strings Attached's* second single, "It's Gonna Be Me," is released; it hits the No.1 spot on the *Billboard Hot 100* chart for two weeks and spends 25 weeks total rotating spots.

September 19, 2000: The third and final single from *No Strings Attached* is released, "This I Promise You"; it peaks at No. 5 on the *Billboard Hot 100* and spends over 26 weeks on the chart. The song is such a hit, a Spanish-language version "Yo te Voy a Amar," is distributed to international markets and the guys perform it live at the Latin Grammys in 2001.

2001

January 28, 2001: NSYNC is tapped to play the halftime show at Super Bowl XXXV in a showstopper that comes to be known as "The Kings of Rock and Pop," also featuring co-headliners Aerosmith as well as Mary J. Blige, Britney Spears, and Nelly.

May 14, 2001: The first single from NSYNC's upcoming album *Celebrity*, is released, the dance number "Pop." The song peaks on the *Billboard Hot 100* at No. 19 and spends 15 weeks on the chart.

May 23, 2001: NSYNC's PopOdyssey Tour kicks off, a long trek in which they debut half the material from upcoming album *Celebrity*.

July 24, 2001: NSYNC's fourth and (to date) final album, *Celebrity*, is released. In its first week, 1.87 million units are sold, regarded as the second-best debut week for any American album.

August 21, 2001: *Celebrity's* second single, "Gone" is released, peaking on the *Billboard Hot 100* at No. 11, with 24 weeks logged on the chart. It's the first time Justin takes total lead on vocals.

2002

January 14, 2002: *Celebrity's* final single is released, the R&B-inspired "Girlfriend"; it peaks at No. 5 on the *Billboard* charts with 20 weeks total in the rankings.

February 23, 2002: NSYNC performs at a concert for the 2002 Winter Olympics, held in Salt Lake City, Utah.

March 3, 2002: NSYNC embark on their fifth and (to date) final tour, the Celebrity Tour, a stripped-back club affair. The tour ends April 28.

May 2002: The band announces a "scheduled hiatus," intending to go back into the studio in December. Instead, this marks the start of 20-plus years apart.

August 5, 2002: Joey makes his Broadway debut in a production of *Rent* to rave reviews.

November 5, 2002: Just six months after NSYNC announces their hiatus and shortly after breaking things off with Britney, Justin releases his solo debut *Justified*, the start of a lucrative solo journey that has made him one of the biggest stars of all time.

2003

February 23, 2003: NSYNC comes back together for a one-off appearance at the 45th annual Grammy Awards to offer a tribute to the Bee Gees.

2004

February 24, 2004: JC releases his one and only solo album, *Schizophrenic*, and while critics love the diversity of music styles on the tracks, it peaks at No. 17 and only spends four weeks on the chart in total.

2007

June 14, 2007: Lou Pearlman is apprehended in Bali and extradited back to the US, where he is sentenced to 300 months in prison.

October 23, 2007: Lance publishes his *New York Times* bestselling memoir, *Out of Sync*.

2010

Chris releases an album with new alt rock band, Nigel's 11.

2013

August 25, 2013: NSYNC reunites for one night only at the 2013 VMAs at the request of Justin himself to celebrate him receiving the Michael Jackson Video Vanguard Award. It's their first time performing together in 10 years.

2016

August 19, 2016: Lou Pearlman dies in prison of a heart attack.

2018

April 30, 2018: NSYNC receives their star on the Hollywood Walk of Fame.

2019

March 2019: *The Boy Band Con: The Lou Pearlman Story* premieres at the prestigious SXSW Film Festival.

April 14, 2019: Four-fifths of NSYNC (everyone but Justin) join Ariana Grande for her headlining performance at Coachella.

2023

September 12, 2023: NSYNC again show up in an unannounced surprise appearance at the MTV VMAs to give Taylor Swift the award for best pop song.

September 14, 2023: Two days after the VMAs, NSYNC announce they are going to release their first new song in 20 years "Better Place," for the *Trolls Band Together* soundtrack.

DISCOGRAPHY

NSYNC

(European version)

Original Release Date:
  May 26, 1997
Record Label: BMG Ariola
  Munich/Trans Continental

SINGLES:
"I Want You Back"
  (January 4, 1997)
"Tearin' Up My Heart"
  (February 10, 1997)
"Here We Go"
  (May 5, 1997)
"For The Girl Who
  Has Everything"
  (August 18, 1997)
"Together Again"
  (November 8, 1997)

Producers: Denniz Pop,
  Max Martin, Veit Renn,
  Kristian Lundin

Sales: Information unavailable

NSYNC

(American version)

Original Release Date:
  March 24, 1998
Record Label:
  BMG/RCA/Trans Continental

SINGLES:
"I Want You Back"
  (January 20, 1998)
"Tearin' Up My Heart"
  (June 30, 1998)
"(God Must Have Spent) A
  Little More Time On You"
  (February 9, 1999)
"Thinking of You (I Drive
  Myself Crazy)"
  (February 15, 1999)

Producers: Denniz Pop,
Max Martin, Veit Renn,
Kristian Lundin, Carl Sturken,
Evan Rogers

Sales: 10 million copies

Home for Christmas

Original Release Date:
  November 10, 1998
Record Label:
  BMG/RCA/Trans Continental

SINGLES:
"Merry Christmas,
  Happy Holidays"
  (November 24, 1998)

Producers: Veit Renn,
  Carl Sturken, Evan
  Rogers, Gary Carolla

Sales: 2 million copies

No Strings Attached

Original Release Date:
   March 21, 2000
Record Label: Jive

SINGLES:
"Bye Bye Bye"
   (January 17, 2000)
"It's Gonna Be Me"
   (May 16, 2000)
"This I Promise You"
   (September 19, 2000)

Producers: Veit Renn, Kristian
   Lundin, Andreas Carlsson,
   Teddy Riley, JC Chasez,
   Justin Timberlake

Sales: 11 million copies

Celebrity

Original Release Date:
   July 24, 2001
Record Label: Jive

SINGLES:
"Pop"
   (May 14, 2001)
"Gone"
   (August 21, 2001)
"Girlfriend"
   (January 14, 2002)

Producers: BT, The Neptunes,
   Kristian Lundin, Wade
   Robson, JC Chasez, Justin
   Timberlake

Sales: 5 million copies

SOLO DISCOGRAPHIES

Note: All sales figures are US-based on certified numbers from RIAA.

Justin Timberlake

Justified

Original Release Date:
 November 5, 2002
Record Label: Jive

SINGLES:
"Like I Love You" (September
 16, 2002)
"Cry Me a River" (November 25,
 2002)
"Rock Your Body" (March 17,
 2003)
"Señorita" (July 7, 2003)

Producers: The Neptunes,
 Timbaland, Scott Storch,
 Brian McKnight

Sales: 3 million copies

FutureSex/ LoveSounds

Original Release Date:
 September 8, 2006
Record Label: Jive

SINGLES:
"SexyBack" (July 18, 2006)
"My Love" (October 24, 2006)
"What Goes Around...Comes
 Around" (December 19,
 2006)
"Summer Love" (April 1, 2007)
"LoveStoned" (June 5, 2007)
"Until The End of Time"
 (October 3, 2007)

Producers: Justin Timberlake,
 Timbaland, Danja,
 Jawbreakers, Rick Rubin

Sales: 4 million copies

The 20/20 Experience

Original Release Date:
 March 15, 2013
Record Label: RCA

SINGLES:
"Suit & Tie" (January 15, 2013)
"Mirrors" (February 11, 2013)
"Tunnel Vision" (June 14, 2003)

Producers: Justin Timberlake,
 Timbaland, Rob Knox, The
 Tennessee Kids, Jerome
 Harmon

Sales: 2 million copies

The 20/20 Experience – 2 Of 2

Original Release Date:
    September 27, 2013
Record Label: RCA

SINGLES:
"Take Back The Night"
    (July 12, 2013)
"TKO" (September 20, 2013)
"Not a Bad Thing"
    (February 24, 2014)
"Drink You Away"
    (November 23, 2015)

Producers: Justin Timberlake,
    Timbaland, Rob Knox,
    Jerome Harmon,
    Daniel Jones

Sales: 1 million copies

Man of the Woods

Original Release Date:
    February 2, 2018
Record Label: RCA

SINGLES:
"Filthy" (January 5, 2018)
"Supplies" (January 18, 2018)
"Say Something"
    (January 25, 2018)
"Man of the Woods"
    (February 2, 2018)

Producers: Justin Timberlake,
    Timbaland, The Neptunes,
    Danja, Eric Hudson, Elliott
    Ives, Larrance Dopson,
    Rob Knox, Jerome Harmon

Sales: 1 million copies

Everything I Thought It Was

Original Release Date:
    March 15, 2024
Record Label: RCA

SINGLES:
"Selfish" (January 25, 2024)
"No Angels" (March 15, 2024)

Producers: Justin Timberlake,
    Timbaland, Ryan Tedder,
    Louis Bell, Cirkut, Andrew
    DeRoberts, Danja,
    Rob Knox, Angel López,
    Frederico Vindver

Sales: No data as of print date

JC Chasez

Schizophrenic

Original Release Date:
    February 24, 2004
Record Label: Jive

SINGLES:
"Some Girls
    (Dance with Women)"
    (November 11, 2003)
"All Day Long I Dream
    About Sex" (October 8, 2004)

Producers: JC Chasez, Dallas
    Austin, Basement Jaxx,

NSYNC at the 2001 Teen Choice Awards.

ACKNOWLEDGMENTS

To every music fan who has wished, hoped, and prayed for their favorite band to come back around again and wears out their CDs and cassette tapes—you are the heart and soul of the music industry. And to my cousins Sarah and Maggie, who joined me early on in the boy band fandom.

ABOUT THE AUTHOR

SELENA FRAGASSI is a 15-year music journalist who is currently a regular contributor for the *Chicago Sun-Times* and previously wrote *New Kids On The Block 40th Anniversary Celebration.* Her byline has also appeared in *SPIN, Loudwire, The A.V. Club, Paste, Nylon, Popmatters, Blurt, Under the Radar*, and *Chicago Magazine* where she was previously on staff as the Pop/Rock Critic. Selena's work has been anthologized in *That Devil Music: Best Music Writing* and she has appeared on televised panels regarding music matters for WTTW's *Chicago Tonight*. She is also a member of the Recording Academy.

IMAGE CREDITS

INDEX

First published in 2024 by Epic Ink, an imprint of The Quarto Group,
142 West 36th Street, 4th Floor, New York, NY 10018, USA
(212) 779-4972 • www.Quarto.com

Epic Ink titles are also available at discount for retail, wholesale, promotional, and bulk purchase. For details, contact the Special Sales Manager by email at specialsales@quarto.com or by mail at The Quarto Group, Attn: Special Sales Manager, 100 Cummings Center Suite 265D, Beverly, MA 01915 USA.

10 9 8 7 6 5 4 3 2 1

ISBN: 978-0-7603-9223-2

Digital edition published in 2024
eISBN: 978-0-7603-8986-7

Library of Congress Control Number: 2024936858

Group Publisher: Rage Kindelsperger
Creative Director: Laura Drew
Managing Editor: Cara Donaldson
Editor: Katie McGuire
Text: Selena Fragassi
Cover and Interior Design: Scott Richardson and Kegley Design

Printed in China